A Beard
in Nepal

A Beard
in Nepal

Fiona Roberts

BOOKS

Winchester, UK
Washington, USA

First published by O-Books, 2012
O-Books is an imprint of John Hunt Publishing Ltd., Laurel House, Station Approach,
Alresford, Hants, SO24 9JH, UK
office1@jhpbooks.net
www.johnhuntpublishing.com

For distributor details and how to order please visit the 'Ordering' section on our website.

ISBN: 978 1 78099 675 2

A CIP catalogue record for this book is available from the British Library.

Design: Stuart Davies

Printed and bound by CPI Group (UK) Ltd, Croydon, CR0 4YY

We operate a distinctive and ethical publishing philosophy in all
areas of our business, from our global network of authors to
production and worldwide distribution.

Contents

Chapter One

Tod's expression wasn't exactly enthusiastic when I told him I'd booked us a two-week trek in Nepal, but I expected to encounter a bit of resistance, my schemes usually did at first.

"It'll be great," I told him, flapping my arms about, "just think of all that healthy exercise, the wonderful views, and the Yaks and monasteries...."

He looked at me with a mixture of amusement and pity, probably more amusement this time around, although it was a close run thing.

"Two weeks trekking through the Himalayas? *The Himalayas*? Who are you kidding?" he said, "Anyway, where *is* Nepal?"

"It's sort of India way," I said, feeling vague. He can be so hurtful sometimes, but I ignored his lack of enthusiasm, it was usually just a front anyway, and settled back in my chair to make one of my lists.

I'd got as far as

1. Walking boots
2. Sleeping bags

and was dithering over sleeping bag liners – would we need them? What did "considerably colder at night" mean? – when an email arrived from Emma.

Emma runs a small Fair Trade company called Hatti Trading which does business with Nepal, and she extends an invitation to her customers each year to go trekking with her in the Himalayas. As a past customer of Hatti Trading that was how I had booked our trek.

So expecting this email to be another update on arrangements for our forthcoming trip, I opened it. It told me that Emma had been asked to try to find a volunteer English teacher for a village school in Nepal.

"Huummm! Interesting," I thought, and emailed her back to say I'd had fourteen years experience as a TEFL (Teacher of English as a Foreign Language) teacher, although that was twenty years ago.

Minutes later another email popped into my inbox. Speedy things, aren't they, emails? Sort of electronic pigeons. I came late to the electronic revolution and haven't really caught up yet.

Emma wrote, "When you've finished the two-week trek why don't I take you up to the village of Salle in the Everest region of Nepal, and leave you there for five months? You can teach English in the school there. Bring Tod too."

"I'd love to," I sent back.

Good-oh. Life was becoming interesting again.

I went in search of my significant other half and found him standing on the outhouse roof. He was glaring at something he called 'Stick and Lick' which, when applied, was supposed to stop all leaks through the roof. But it didn't seem to be sticking *or* licking at that moment, and judging by the look on Tod's face it didn't know how much trouble it was in.

"Huummm. This could go either way," I thought, "I'll try the subtle approach."

"Hello, dear," I called up to him, "Bit of a change of plan. We're going to Nepal for five months now, and I'll be teaching in a village school after the trek. You're ok with that, aren't you?"

One of the things I love about Tod is his unflappability. He *is* getting rather deaf though, and that's probably why he said,

"*What!*" in quite a loud voice.

"Five months, dear," I repeated, "You're self-employed so you can give yourself the time off can't you? You only have to ask nicely."

He stared at me with rather an odd, unfamiliar expression on his face.

"Can I take that as a yes?" I called.

Tod nodded slowly and mumbled something in my direction

which sounded like, "It wouldn't make any difference *what* I said," but I'm sure it wasn't that, because we always discuss my ideas before we tackle them.

"Goody," I said, "I'll go and make a list."

So that's how it happened that Tod and I went to Nepal for five months.

Perhaps we seem unlikely adventurers. Neither of us is in the first flush of youth, and I was something like two stone overweight at the time. I wasn't exactly as fit as a butcher's dog either, or any tradesman's dog actually, but Emma said the trek would be 'medium difficult', and then how hard could it be, I thought, living in a small village in the mountains for the following four months? I decided to go for it.

Tod was pretty fit physically, and once he'd realised that I was serious about this latest adventure, he was almost as excited about it as I was. Well, almost.

I work two days a week in an office. I love the work, and personally I wouldn't have described my request for five months unpaid leave of absence as 'unreasonable', but it wouldn't do if we were all the same, would it? Our trip hung in the balance for several nail-biting weeks, but then, albeit grudgingly, permission was eventually forthcoming.

So, full of renewed enthusiasm for our adventure I began to try to collect as much information as I could about the village, the school, and the Everest region of Nepal. But I was surprised at just how little I managed to find out, and although I trawled the internet for hours at a time, what I finally ended up with would have fitted neatly onto the back of a ten Nepali Rupee note.

The village of Salle (pronounced Solley) is roughly twenty kilometres from the small town of Jiri. Jiri was, but no longer is, Everest's Base Camp, and is about two hundred kilometres north east of Kathmandu. It was from here that the great Edmund Hillary set out on his successful expedition to conquer Everest.

Salle is about two thousand metres above sea level, situated in a valley amongst the mountains of the Everest region.

I discovered that the only water available in the village came from one small pipe. I also discovered that we would not be able to drink that water, or eat anything that had been washed in it. Odd, I thought. Why would water, seemingly uncontaminated, coming directly from a small mountain stream fed by a glacier in a remote area of Nepal, be so dangerous to our health? But I was reliably informed that the miniscule meanies in that water would do us untold damage. Humm. P'raps better not mention that one to Tod just yet. A softly softly approach might be best for the moment.

Surprisingly, electricity reaches the village, but only enough to power one small light bulb per dwelling. Better add candles to the list, and get an eyesight check up before we go, I thought.

It seemed there were two schools in or near Salle, a Junior and a Secondary, but I could not discover anything about the children's levels of English language, or indeed how many children attended those schools.

I visited friends in the UK who still teach in Language schools, and picked their brains about up to date teaching methods. Had anything changed, I wondered, since *my* teaching days? It was fun brushing up and looking through the masses of new material that was available to today's language teachers.

As time went on and our departure date drew nearer, friends and colleagues began to make concerned noises about a potentially dangerous lack of information about our destination; about the obvious lack of sanitation; lack of safe drinking water, and the dangers inherent in a lengthy trip to such a remote area of the world.

I already knew that Nepal was one of the planet's poorest countries, but I didn't mention to Tod that it also has an abysmal record of road transport safety – he's a biker, and is very aware of road safety. Need to know only, I decided. P'raps better not mention *that* fact just yet either.

Our front room began to fill up with piles of trekking socks; his and her thermals; four season sleeping bags; trekking food for Tod; filter water bottles; solar battery chargers; medication; solar torches........

The list of inoculations we needed seemed endless, and of course some of them were only available privately and at considerable cost. Following our second of three rabies inoculations the nurse rang us in a panic,

"Are you ok?" she asked, somewhat breathlessly, "Only, there should have been at least a *two*-week gap between the rabies injections, not just one week."

"I'll call Tod," I said, "He's just at the window barking at the neighbours, but I'll get him to ring you back."

We weathered that particular storm, and strode bravely on to the next.

I read up on altitude sickness. We'd visited Peru four years earlier and I'd suffered from it badly then. I remembered I'd sworn never again to expose myself to its effects. Huummm. *How* high was the village?

The internet informed me that a limited amount of medication was available that just might help mitigate the worst effects of altitude. Another private prescription.

All of a sudden we were ready. Tod packed our rucksacks. We filled up to the absolute limit with stuff for the schools – books; pens; pencils; posters.

We said goodbye to everyone here, and I noted a curious similarity running through our friends' expressions as they wished us well. It was a sort of astonished wonder – I was rather hurt. Were we really such unlikely intrepid adventurers?

At least Tod looked the part even if **I** didn't. His long, bushy beard and shoulder length hair had turned greyish over the past couple of years – he looked a bit as if he'd been living in a cave.

I wondered what they'd make of Tod's beard in Nepal.

Chapter Two

Our great adventure didn't start too well. I couldn't lift my rucksack and whinged until Tod picked both rucksacks up and carried them to the car.

I was actually finding just the small hand-luggage backpack a bit of a struggle. This didn't bode well.

The flight to Kathmandu was fine, and we were relieved to find that our luggage had accompanied us on the trip. Our excitement grew as we met up with Emma outside the airport.

It was only a short taxi ride to our hotel in the tourist area of the city, but it was long enough to form the opinion that Kathmandu is an 'in your face' kind of place. There just didn't seem to be room enough for everyone and everything that was trying to squash onto the roads – cars; trucks; motorbikes; rickshaws; people; cows; piles of rubbish....

That well-remembered short first trip was a jaw-dropping experience.

Over the next three days the other eight members of our trekking group arrived. They were great, and we all got along really well. We were looking forward to the trek.

Emma introduced us to Dhan, the Nepalese man who would be our guide during the trek. He actually came from the village of Salle, where Tod and I would be spending several months, so we thought we'd be able to get some more information from him about the village and the schools. But no.

"Don't worry," he said, "You don't need to know anything now. I'll take you up to the village and introduce you to everyone there after the trek."

I felt a bit like a mushroom, kept in the dark. I hoped my forward planning was going to be adequate.

We drove out of Kathmandu in a mini bus on the first day of the trek. Apparently they drive on the left in Nepal, but you'd be forgiven for not immediately realising that, or even for thinking that a decision on sides was still pending.

In Kathmandu, away from the city centre the roads are mostly very narrow, overhung by crumbling buildings, and filled with potholes, stray bricks, and dust. It remains one of the great mysteries of the universe how so much can fit into such a confined space. It is constant noisy chaos, and is pretty easy to get squashed on the roads there by any number of vehicles. And the people, those wonderful Nepalese people in colourful clothes, laughing and shouting, scurrying here and there, great swathes of them milling around or crowded noisily together on corners. We were fascinated. Everywhere we walked people would call friendly greetings to us.

Driving out of Kathmandu valley the roads become little more than narrow uneven tracks filled with potholes, generous amounts of rubble (where on earth does it all come from?), cracks, bumps, and totally manic drivers whose ears and eyes must surely be tuned into a parallel universe.

These narrow roads climb high up the sides of the valley and are mostly hewn out of the mountains themselves, clinging to the edges, impossibly high up. In places the road has collapsed completely following landslides, and the jumbled rubble trails down the steep mountain sides, reminding you how easy it would be to slip down with it.

I had never driven along such high roads. Did you know that the safety barrier hasn't yet been invented in Nepal? You are right there, sitting right on the edge of the drop. Even a careful driver would have his work cut out to stay on the road, especially amongst the hoards of undeniably deranged truck drivers, and suicidal car drivers.

It was a six-hour drive to Pokhara, Nepal's second city, in sweltering thirty-something degree heat. At the best of times driving in Nepal is not a restful affair, and we constantly crashed down holes, hit bricks, and avoided cows, people and other vehicles as we bumped and slithered along.

Twenty minutes ahead of us a Local Bus skidded off the road and plunged a thousand feet, maybe more, down to the ravine floor, landing on its roof beside the softly flowing, disinterested river. When we drove past, a small group of local people were standing at the edge of the sheer drop, staring down at what remained of the bus far below. It was all they could do. Rescue was out of the question. Their brightly coloured clothes looked oddly out of place in that grim spot.

We were told that there is a huge problem of Local Bus drivers drinking raxi, the locally distilled firewater, before getting behind the wheel. But these kinds of accident are so common in Nepal that they provoke just a bit of a shrug, and ten minutes of noticeably more careful driving by passing vehicles. Life then resumes its normal chaotic style.

We began the trek through the Annapurna region the next day. Few things in life are certain, but to 'death' and 'taxes' I will add that never, ever again will I trek through the Himalayas, or anywhere at all for that matter....

Anyone who has done that trek, and it is the most popular one with British tourists, will know what I am talking about!

Tod was fantastic. He hardly broke into a sweat at any time. He's a biker – what do you expect? I, on the other hand, spent the entire week slipping, falling, stumbling, tripping and sliding all over the charmingly steep stone steps of the beautiful, nay spectacular, Annapurna region. There were times when I just could not put one shaky foot in front of the other, I was completely exhausted. Speech was out of the question for me most of the time – I couldn't spare the breath. It was not the altitude that did for me, but just the sheer physical effort of the ascent. Oh boy, was I ever unfit! One of the things that drove me on was the thought of how many friends and colleagues would say, "Told you so!" if I gave up. So I struggled sweatily on.

We trekked up to 6,000ft on the first day, 9,000ft on the second day, and apparently 11,000ft on the third day, by which time I was considering throwing myself off the mountain, as a much better alternative to having to slip, slide, fall or stumble back down those steps again.

I now have a permanent imprint of Tod's hand on my posterior, as he literally shoved me up, step after step. It is testament to his good nature that he never said; "Told you so!" although I'm sure that was on the tip of his tongue many times.

I nearly fainted when we started trudging through *snow*. We had been caught in a hailstorm (they were not your small 'doesn't hurt if it hits you' type stones either), drenched in spectacularly heavy rain, and frazzled by hot sunshine on the way up the mountains, so when we actually reached the *snowline* you can imagine I was beside myself with joy.

I have never seen such mountain goats as the Nepalese porters who accompanied us on the trek, and (the clue's in the name) carried our rucksacks for us. We were all full of admiration for them as they flitted past us up those accursed mountain steps, and this with a *couple* of our rucksacks on their backs. *I* couldn't even carry *one*. We're talking two or three feet rise between stone steps you know, not your barely noticeable, take it in your stride, common or garden English doorstep....

Every time I slipped a couple of the porters would appear beside me as if by magic, grabbing the appropriate flailing limb to stop me catapulting into space. They always reached me just in time – amazing. They'd shout to each other, and then one or two of them would be there picking me up again.

After a few days someone told me what they shouted to each other:

"Catch the English teacher!"

"Don't lose the English teacher!"

Right-oh. Some vested interests I can live with.

Eventually I had two porters more or less permanently attached to my arms. They'd upgraded me to two after I nearly took one with me off a rope and wood slat bridge slung over a ravine. I mistimed the swaying about bit.

The porters were only small, but thank God for their vice-like grip.

Different shape, more hair, longer ears, but definitely on a par strength-wise were the mountain donkeys. As you can imagine, up in the mountains anything you don't grow or make there has to be carried up the mountain to you. We were warned to get out of the donkeys' way whenever we heard a group of them coming up or down the trail – the three lead donkeys wear lots of large, deep-sounding bells so you can hear them coming from a mile away.

The first time we encountered a donkey train we all obediently scurried to the edge of the track and breathed in. Just in time the porters, waiting further up the mountain, spotted we were all standing on the wrong side, with our backs to the sheer drop, and they rushed down and dragged us across to the other side, just as the lead donkeys trotted past.

Good move. The donkeys were wearing double panniers with heavy calor gas bottles in them. They would neatly have popped us all over the edge of the mountain like skittles, without even noticing.

Would you believe that the donkey trains don't require a human to tell them what to do, or which way to go. The lead donkeys trot along the trail for a while and then just stop, stock still, until all the stragglers catch up and they have a breather. Then off they go again. How wonderful is that?

We descended a mile in altitude in one day – that included the notorious 3,280 stone steps that any trekking tourist who has visited the Annapurna region of Nepal will recall, and then we walked another four miles or so to the edge of the beautiful lake at Pokhara, and the end of our trek.

Frankly, by the time I got there I couldn't have cared less if it was a beautiful lake or not – it could have been a pig sty for all I cared at that moment. Nothing against pig sties, but I have never been so glad to finish anything. Surely I can't be alone in this? I can't be the only overweight and unfit tourist ever to have been foolish enough to think that the Annapurna trek would be a doddle?

Tod loved every moment of it, and could probably have done double the trek distance. Our own porters, and almost every other Nepalese porter or guide that we met along the way called him 'Ali Baba', because of his beard. They were absolutely fascinated by it, having little or no facial hair themselves. They all wanted to touch it. Everywhere we went, as soon as they spotted Tod's beard adults and children alike called, "Hello, Ali Baba!" and there was always much laughter, which Tod joined in with. He loved it. If you should ever need an ice-breaker in Nepal, grow a beard!

I felt rather cheated that we hadn't seen a Yak during the trek, as Yak-watching featured high on my list of things to do in Nepal. Mind you, we did see half a Yak. The porters said the creature in question *was* a Yak, but Tod was sure it wasn't. As far as he was concerned it was a 'Cow-Yak' – yes, they *do* exist. Anyway, as it was lying down behind a tree, and didn't obligingly stand up, I couldn't check out if it had very hairy legs – a sure fire way to check Yakkiness apparently. So Yak-watching remained unticked on my list, and would have to wait for a more appropriate moment, which as it turned out was our trip to Tibet.

Chapter Three

At the end of the trek, before we went back to Kathmandu and then on to the village of Salle, Tod and I decided to spend three days sightseeing in Chitwan National Park. This is a hot, jungle area of Nepal on the Indian border, well-known to British visitors. We were told we would see wild rhinos, crocodiles, an elephant breeding centre, and a vast array of colourful birds.

We were really looking forward to it, me especially, as it marked the end of the indignity of dragging myself up and down mountains, slipping and falling all over the place, and arriving last everywhere, red in the face and out of breath -- at least for the moment anyway.

All we had to do to get to Chitwan was to subject ourselves to six hours of being thrown around in a Local Bus as it swerved, skidded, stopped unexpectedly and inexplicably, crashed into potholes, and hit rocks and rubble on the road.

Then, to add to all that, there'd be the Nepalese music in the bus, very loud, *all* the time. Oh joy. Getting into any bus, anywhere in Nepal, magically triggers the music, and any subsequent conversation has to be carried out in a shout, or not at all. I never got used to this.

The journey went pretty much according to expectation, and on arrival in the Chitwan region we stepped down from the bus into a breathtaking wall of dusty heat, and a noisy mob of local jeep drivers, all trying to find their fares to half a dozen different hotels.

We grabbed our rucksacks which had been unceremoniously chucked down from the roof of the bus, scurried away from the melee, and sat down on them to wait for our hotel jeep-driver to find us.

In stark contrast to the Annapurna region which we'd just left, Chitwan was flat, and spread out around us, through the heat haze we could see field after field of neatly cultivated crops, clusters of trees here and there, and villages. Leaving aside the ongoing scrum in front of us there was a noticeably peaceful and relaxed feeling here.

One by one the jeeps loaded up with their cargoes of eager tourists and shot off along the road, leaving dust trails hanging unsteadily behind them in the hot air. Eventually one of the few remaining drivers ambled over to us and said,

"Royal Park Hotel?"

"Yes," we said, picked up our rucksacks and carried them over to the open backed jeep. It already contained two passengers, and I recognised them immediately as the couple who'd got on the bus in a remote village along the way. I had particularly noticed them for two reasons, the first being that I didn't know the language they spoke. It was totally unfamiliar to me. The second reason is considerably more delicate, and please forgive me if you feel I'm being cruel here.

You'll have heard the expression, 'As God made them so He matched them'?

Well, never was that expression so appropriate as with this couple.

They were both very short, maybe just a whisker over five feet, and they were both very dumpy. They matched perfectly. They'd have made great book ends.

We climbed into the jeep, said hello to them, and then off we went, racing along the straight, dusty road towards a village glimpsed in the distance.

It was an exhilarating ride; the hot, dusty air took your breath away, and we passed elephants helping out in the fields, and camels plodding slowly along the sun baked road (snooty creatures, aren't they?).

Our hotel was just what you'd expect to find in the tourist area of a jungle – a group of small thatched huts spaced around a communal bar and dining area. There were jungley-type trees and vegetation, and loud, brightly coloured wildlife everywhere.

After lunch we clambered into a small ox-cart and set off in the baking heat for a leisurely tour of the village and surrounding area. We passed half a dozen small shops, their smiling owners sitting outside in groups. They laughed and waved to us. We passed groups of locals walking along the roads or working in the fields. They all smiled and waved to us. Tod's beard was much admired, and the now familiar cries of, "Hello, Ali Baba!" followed us everywhere.

"It's a really happy, laid back place, isn't it?" I said to Tod.

No answer.

"It feels really peaceful, doesn't it?" I said.

"You could say that," he said.

Bit of an odd thing to say, I thought. I looked across at him but Tod was looking out over the fields, a thoughtful expression on his face. He didn't look at me. On we went along narrow tracks with overgrowing greenery cascading down and brushing both sides of the cart.

"This is great," I said.

I caught hold of a passing small branch and broke it off.

"This smells strange," I said, wafting the leaves in front of Tod's nose, "You can smell this everywhere, and look, it's growing all over the place. I wonder what it is. There's a whole field of it over there, and it's in all the hedgerows." I looked round, wondering.

Tod was grinning, "It's marijuana," he said.

"Don't be daft," I said.

"Seriously," he said, "it's marijuana."

I tapped the ox-cart driver on the shoulder. He looked round and I noted a suspiciously wide grin on his face. Before I could say anything he nodded towards the sprig of greenery in my hand and said,

"Yes, marijuana," and his grin grew even wider as he turned back to the business of driving the cart.

I'm not a prude, far from it, but I have to say I was actually dumbfounded.

"Look at it all!" I squeaked, "It's *everywhere*! You can smell it all over the place."

Huummm.... How could you live in the middle of all this aroma and not be affected by it? Actually, how could you still be walking straight?

I started to look more closely at the locals. I began to check out the ox-cart drivers to see if they were singing 'Mr Tambourine Man' into their ox's ears.

Were the elephant drivers having a crafty drag on a joint from behind the shelter of a large ear? *And what about the animals?* Was that snooty camel actually smiling at me?

Tod found it all really funny.

At dinner later that evening we shared a table with a pleasant, young Swiss woman. She was in Nepal for three months doing voluntary work.

"Are you going on the dug-out canoe trip to look for crocodiles?" she asked us.

We told her we intended going the next day.

"I've been on the trip twice. Let me know what you think about the crocodile," she said.

"We might not see one," we said.

"You will!" she said.

Odd, we thought.

The next morning we walked down to the river and stood waiting for the dug-outs to arrive. The intense heat seemed to accentuate the calm quiet of the day. By this time my nose had developed a life of its own, and had become a kind of marijuana-seeking device. Every time it detected a whiff of that substance on the warm air I'd nudge Tod. He just grinned.

We'd never been in a jungle before, and we both found it fascinating. The part of the river that we'd come to marked the beginning of the jungle, and from here it quietly wended its way along between high banks overflowing with thick, lush greenery. The clear water appeared quite deep in places. While we waited the guide gave us a few handy hints:

Once you are seated in the dug-out don't move about or we'll all fall in.

Don't allow your hand to touch the water or it may be eaten.

Never speak above a whisper or you may attract the unwanted attention of a crocodile.

Right-oh. Got the idea.

Eventually a couple of long, narrow, wooden boats arrived, looking very much like what I imagined North American Indian canoes to look like.

Very carefully, particularly so in my case, we climbed into the dug-out. The guide sat at the front, then Tod, myself, the Dumpy couple, and finally the chap with the pole thing to push us along.

Off we went. It was great. So quiet and peaceful. The air that hung above the river seemed pristine, almost velvety.

Every so often something jungley would squark or screech from the river bank, and we'd all smile and nod to each other as if we knew exactly what type of creature had made that sound,

"Yes, yes, definitely the Lesser Spotted Womblebat, nod, nod, arf, arf...."

The river was silently fast flowing, and in one or two places you could see the bottom. We spotted a few shoals of very small fish ambling about, but no piranha, and nothing remotely resembling a crocodile. After half an hour I started to smile each time the guide turned round to us and put his finger to his lips, dramatically hushing us to silence. Not that anyone was speaking. We weren't. We were all too spellbound by the silent jungle scenery.

Suddenly the guide bellowed, *Crocodile! Over there!*

"Oh my God!" I said to Tod as he handed me my sunglasses which had parted company with my face as I jumped in fright, "I thought we weren't supposed to attract attention," I was peeved.

"Well, *he* doesn't look in the least bit interested," Tod said, pointing towards the crocodile in question, apparently sunning himself on the river bank.

He was one of those with the long pointy noses, and must have been about eight or nine feet long. His front and back right feet were casually submerged in the water, and I assumed he was keeping still so he'd blend in and we wouldn't notice him. I stared, enthralled. I'd never seen a crocodile up close before. He didn't move a muscle as we floated past, gawping.

"Don't worry," the guide said in a loud, theatrical whisper, "We're safe," and he patted the pistol he wore at his waist.

"Too right we're safe," Tod whispered to me, "I've never heard of a plastic crocodile attacking anyone."

I looked over at the creature on the river bank and knew instantly that Tod was right. I just knew it. Either he was a very old, arthritic crocodile, moth-eaten in places along his back, and with one loose eye, or he was made of severely weather beaten plastic.

We played along and tried hard not to giggle, but when a second cry of, "*Crocodile!*" rang out it was all we could do not to laugh out loud. This time it was just a crocodile head, yes, a head, detached from any body, floating in the river, nose stuck into the mud of the side bank to keep it steady, hanging there.

Right-oh.

The rest of the river trip was pretty uneventful in comparison. The guide drew our attention to a lot of shaking foliage at one point, and told us it was caused by a colony of rare monkeys. We *did* wickedly consider it might have been a few rope pulling locals instead, but we saw neither rare monkey nor sneaky local, so we'll never know about that one.

We sought out the young Swiss woman at lunch time, and before a word was said we all burst into laughter.

"You'd think they'd move it a bit from time to time, to give the impression it's alive," she said, still giggling.

But none of us felt even remotely annoyed or cheated, and in fact we could understand what had probably motivated the plastic croc scenario. We had an example ourselves. During the trek a group of tourists (not British, I hasten to say) had given their Nepalese guide a very hard time because the weather was bad, and they couldn't see the mountain views they'd expected to see. They actually seemed to consider their guide was to blame for Nature's choice of weather that day. So our plastic crocodile was doubtless motivated by a desire on the guides' part to avoid a similar outburst.

After lunch we decided to go for an 'Elephant Safari', which we supposed would be just an elephant ride. How wrong could we be?

I'm not particularly in favour of animal rides, but there is a well-publicised elephant breeding centre in Chitwan, and those elephants we'd seen so far looked fit and happy, as far as we could tell. We decided to give the 'Elephant Safari' a go.

We found ourselves standing in line behind the Dumpies. By now we'd discovered they were Catalonian, and although we couldn't communicate with them other than by smiles and gestures, we knew they were nice people.

Each waiting elephant had a square seat on his back, large enough for four tourists to sit in. However, we had to get up there first.

Our elephant was standing beside a wobbly wooden structure which was our get on board method. It wasn't easy to climb, and Tod had to drag me up the last bit. By the time I was in launch position on the platform at the top, the Dumpies were already in the seat, waiting.

Now, there's not a great deal of space in a four-seater elephant chair, and as Tod and I looked down into ours we couldn't see any at all, because the Dumpies had spread into every corner of it and were sitting smiling innocently up at us.

To this day I do not know how we managed to join the

Dumpies in the seat. But a couple of minutes later, with all four of us wedged rigid on top, our elephant set off after six or seven others, which obviously had less statistically challenged occupants in their seats.

I had not immediately noticed that no one was driving our elephant. Wedged as I was at the back of the seat I had a great view of where we'd been, tail included, but not where we were going. So it came as a bit of a surprise when a grinning face literally popped up, and hovered in the air at the back of the elephant.

"Hello. I take you for nice ride," it said. He was standing on the elephant's foot, which the placid creature had obligingly raised.

When you get a chance have a look at an elephant's foot. Amazing. Toe nails like barn doors.

Our driver hopped on board and away we went, plodding slowly through the small village and out into the countryside towards the jungle.

I have to say I was not comfortable. The odd kind of swaying movement didn't agree with me, and as we were tightly wedged together with the Dumpies, we all swayed exactly in unison. We must have looked like one of those wind-up toy horses with rigid plastic riders on top. We swayed uncomfortably into the jungle.

Our driver was full of fun. He sat backwards on the elephant and chatted to us.

Ahead we could hear lots of talking, giggling, and the occasional roar of laughter floating back on the still air from the rest of the group. Everyone was having a good time.

We plodded along the jungle paths, ducking to avoid hanging vines, and laughing when we saw two elephants racing each other, their drivers yelling and laughing, the tourists hanging on for dear life, having a great time.

And then suddenly we were in a clearing. There, in the middle of the grassy open space, we could see a family of wild rhinos – mother, father and tiny replica baby.

The elephants walked slowly around and stood within a few yards of the rhinos, allowing us marvelling tourists a fantastic view of the beautiful wild creatures.

Our driver suddenly appeared below us on the ground – he had slid down the elephant's trunk.

"Give me your cameras. I'll take photos of you," he called up. He caught my camera neatly – he was obviously expert in the art of catching cameras thrown from elephants – and took quite a few photos.

The other drivers were doing the same, except for the one standing on his elephant's head, and another one who was being thrown up into the air by his elephant's foot, and landing back on it to enthusiastic applause from his group of tourists.

They were really putting on a show.

We weren't exactly being quiet, and I looked over at the rhino family to see how they were reacting to this invasion of their previously peaceful privacy.

They continued munching, and hadn't moved from centre stage, seemingly oblivious to us rowdy newcomers.

An elephant lumbered past us, its tourists squealing with laughter. A young European woman was actually steering the elephant while the Nepalese driver sat way back by its tail.

"Look at that!" I said to Tod, "and the rhinos haven't taken any notice of us at all. They're really laid-back."

"They're stoned," Tod said

"Sorry?"

"*Stoned*. Everyone," he said, looking round and grinning.

It occurred to me that he could possibly be right. We both started to giggle. I could well imagine that all the drivers had been on the wacky-backy – you just had to look at them. And what about the elephants and rhinos? Well, there had not been even a wary glance, or backwards step when the first elephant had lumbered into the clearing. It seemed that the heady aroma of marijuana had brought peace and love all around, man.

We couldn't stop giggling.

And then suddenly all the drivers got back up on their elephants amidst cries of,

"Race! Race!" and off we all went, at a trot.

Have you ever had the misfortune to be wedged tightly into a seat on top of a trotting elephant? Oh dear.

We crashed through the jungle, ducking and diving, not always successfully, to avoid hanging vegetation and branches. We seemed to take the wrong path at one stage and found ourselves alone, with the noise of the other elephants' progress receding into the distance. The driver decided to turn our elephant around and go back.

Have you ever been on an elephant in reverse?

Narrow jungle path, thickly growing vegetation along both sides, ropey-type things hanging down across the path, thwacking you in the face....

Reverse gear did not go well.

In the absence of helpful side mirrors our elephant stepped backwards into thick, unyielding foliage which draped itself uncomfortably over myself and the Catalan lady, but wouldn't you know it, hardly touched our male companions.

By the time we'd re engaged first gear Mrs Dumpy and I were covered in sticky, white, cottony-type stuff which immediately began to make us itch.

Wonderful.

Off we went again, and eventually caught up with the others at the river. All the elephants waded into the water together – a truly beautiful sight – and spent some time paddling around enjoying themselves, while we enjoyed the view from a high and dry, though gently swaying distance.

And then we were on our way back. This time we walked sedately through fields of healthy looking crops, with marijuana hedgerows and smiling locals.

Back at the hotel I stood under a cold shower to try to reduce the swollen red blotches all over my face and arms. Mrs Dumpy did the same next door.

Before we left the next day one of the guides took Tod, who is a keen beekeeper, to see the giant wild honey bees. They had colonised part of a building near the hotel, and they were big. Tod was in his element, standing right below the huge cones and taking pictures. I waited at a sensible distance.

We'd really enjoyed our jungle visit, and as we left that part of Nepal to travel north east towards the Everest region, we were conscious that the *real* adventure now lay ahead of us.

Chapter Four

Our intention had been to spend two days in Kathmandu before leaving for the village of Salle. However, we were stranded in the capital city by a transport strike, and didn't actually manage to leave there until the fourth day, by which time we were anxious to get going.

We set off at 7.30am on a ten-seater public mini bus which, Dhan assured us, was marginally a better bet at preserving our lives than a Local Bus would have been. We had an eight-or nine-hour journey in front of us.

Kathmandu 'bus station' (I use this name advisedly) is without doubt a snapshot of hell. Words fail me. You will just have to take my word for it that you wouldn't wish your worst enemy to have to spend any time there. At a later date, on a return visit to Kathmandu, we had reason to venture into the bus station again. I have therefore attempted a description of that place in a later chapter.

Dhan and some of his friends came with us in the mini bus, and the remaining three seats were filled by female Swedish students on their way to Jiri. There they were going to study a rare tree that a certain kind of paper can be made from, and which seems only to grow in the Everest region of Nepal, and in Sweden.

As we ploughed into the swirl of manic traffic on the main road out of Kathmandu going north east, although it was early in the day the temperature had already hit a sweaty thirty degrees. The heat made the already appalling air quality even worse, and we drove through clouds of foul-smelling dust and grime that covered everything, and left a filthy residue in its wake.

Much as we liked Kathmandu, just at that moment we were glad to be leaving.

We could move only very slowly through the masses of cars,

trucks, motorbikes, people and animals moving in swathes across the road, so it took us nearly an hour to start climbing out of Kathmandu valley, through the cloud of grime, to finally reach some semblance of clear air above.

Then of course we were in competition with the manic truckers and alien car drivers, as we screeched round blind corners, overtook, undertook, and just about every other kind of took and, let me remind you, this was a 'good' driver.

Tod and I tried to doze off so we wouldn't be tempted to look out the window and scare ourselves. But the obligatory loud, unfamiliar music in the bus kept us awake. A short time later we had to stop because the villagers from one of the small settlements along the narrow and *only* road had barricaded it. No vehicle was able to pass. This was in protest at lack of funding from the government for water supply to the village. The traffic jam grew larger and larger.

We sat and waited in the clammy heat for two hours, along with seemingly half the population of the Everest region. They didn't complain at all, and simply sat patiently in their vehicles, or at the roadside, and waited, laughing and talking. The only complaints came from our three Swedish travelling companions, but we all ignored them.

And then, roadblock cleared, we were underway again, this time like greyhounds out of traps, and we passengers clung to whatever we could as our driver challenged massive trucks, skidded past cars, and neatly avoided the occasional wandering cow.

Out of the blue, the Swedish girl in the seat behind me hit me on the shoulder.

"Sorry," she said in excellent but heavily accented English, "but something was walking on your shoulder, and it wasn't very nice."

I couldn't see anything, and Tod sitting next to me couldn't either, so we just forgot about it. We drove on (I use the verb loosely) for another couple of hours, and it got hotter and hotter. We were travelling along the Tibet road, and when we reached a certain small, isolated village we needed to turn right, off that road, over a bridge and onto the Jiri Base Camp road.

However, the traffic had got itself into such a jam in the village that we found ourselves completely stationary and trapped, unable to move at all, along with maybe fifty other assorted vehicles, and a few four-legged wanderers. One harassed-looking traffic policeman tried to sort it out, and as with most things in Nepal this was accompanied by much loud talking from all involved.

Once again we settled back to wait.

Then Tod spotted something crawling down the window next to me. It was a cockroach. A nice, deep brown, shiny cockroach.

Now, I'm pretty much ok with cockroaches. I wouldn't say I'd keep one as a pet, but they don't make my skin crawl like spiders do....

However, more and more of them began streaming out from behind the side panel of the bus next to me, and Tod had his work cut out 'removing' them, especially those few which had dropped onto my seat and were dashing up my back and arms.

But we didn't make a fuss, and pretty soon I was cockroach free. The exodus from behind the side panel had stopped, and all was quiet.

When the traffic jam cleared we got going again and were the sixth vehicle to cross the wide bridge, driving slowly between the heavy metal stanchions, nose to tail with others, mostly large trucks, all the way across. We gazed down at the fast flowing river far below.

Coming off the bridge I looked back and saw a large, red-lettered sign roughly nailed to the first stanchion,

'Dangerous Bridge. Cross One Vehicle At A Time'

Right-oh. We may perhaps find that particular bridge absent on our return journey.

An hour or so later we stopped to stretch our legs. As I picked my shoulder bag up from the floor, even without my glasses on, I saw it was crawling, and so were my trousers, with cockroaches. Nice, deep brown, shiny cockroaches.

This time I couldn't help letting out a yelp and leaping over Tod's legs to relative safety, as he started frantically 'removing' the cockroaches from both me and my bag.

"Do not kill them or they will come back!" one of the Swedish girls suddenly said in a loud voice from the back of the small bus. She was glaring across the seats at us.

Unfortunately for her, her accent made that statement sound, well, almost smug, and let's face it she *had* caught me at rather a bad moment in my life. In the interests of Anglo-Swedish relations I resisted the temptation to lean over, pull her out of her seat, and dump her in mine, so we could see how she'd deal with hoards of cockroaches abseiling down her neat jacket and onto her neat trousers.

Instead I glared at her and snapped,

"If we kill them **dead** how are they going to come back?"

Luckily for her she had the wisdom to remain silent, and an international incident was averted.

Dhan jumped into my ex-seat,

"I don't mind cockroaches," he said, and proceeded to prove it over the next 130 kilometres by squishing, squashing, and otherwise removing the by now dwindling hoards. I pretended not to notice. So did the Swedish girl.

We watched the stunning Himalayan scenery through the window for the rest of the trip.

We reached the end of our journey nearly three hours late. Dusk was falling as we stopped at a small group of houses high in the mountains. Dhan told us we would have to walk from here to the village of Salle, but he didn't say how far that was, or how long it might take.

There seemed to be quite a large group of people standing

around watching us as we waited for our rucksacks to be dumped from the top of the bus. By now we'd acquired the knack of packing our rucksacks so that any breakables were well protected, as dumping happens quite a lot in Nepal.

I was hoping that the walk to the village wasn't going to take too long because I was stiff, sore and tired, hungry too, when Dhan appeared in front of us and said,

"These people are from my village. They've come here to welcome you and to walk to Salle with you."

We realised that the waiting crowd had gathered round us, and we could see a lot of tiny children in school uniform amongst them.

"These are some of your pupils," Dhan said.

Many of the children were really very young, maybe four or five years old, and of course because we were late everyone had been waiting for us for nearly three hours. We felt mortified. But there were only welcoming smiles all around us.

Then, with quite a to-do, the village elders made speeches welcoming us to Nepal (Dhan translated for us), and they all came and shook our hands. Everyone cheered as the children lined up and one by one put flower garlands and silk scarves round our necks. Some of the children were so tiny they had to be lifted up. Dhan grabbed our cameras and took photos as the garlands piled higher and higher.

Then the school teachers added their scarves to the rapidly growing piles, and finally the elders came back again to thank us for coming to their village to help their school.

Tod was great. As usual he took it all in his stride, telling everyone to call him Ali Baba because of his beard, which raised an enormous laugh. Adults and children crowded round him, fascinated by the beard, wanting to touch it, staring at it. Most of them had never seen a beard before, let alone one so long and on a white man too. There was a lot of laughter.

I can't say I exactly rose to the occasion. I was stunned by all the attention; I hadn't expected it, and I felt very undeserving of it. For the first time I realised that the villagers regarded our visit as a huge happening in the life of their village, and of the school. Something of the responsibility of it all crept up on me, and just for one moment I wondered if I'd done the right thing by coming here. Was I up to it? Had I given it enough thought? I really hoped I wasn't going to let them all down.

But I didn't have time to muse for long as the crowd started to move off en masse, taking us along with them. In the dim light of the falling dusk I got a fleeting glimpse of a cluster of wood-built dwellings along a rough, muddy road, and then suddenly we were onto a narrow mountain path.

The trek had taught me that I just trip, skid, slide and fall over if I'm not constantly watching where I put my feet. However, try as I might there was absolutely no way I could even *see* my feet at that moment; the garlands and scarves round my neck were just too bulky, and in fact I was forced to look slightly *up* if anything. Anxiously, I tried to solve the potential problem by lifting my feet (in heavy walking boots) higher than usual, and of course my arms were held quite far away from my body for some kind of much needed extra balance.

It didn't take me long to notice, as we processed in a group down the steep, narrow, rough mountain track, that the previously enthusiastic gaggle of little children who'd been walking with me, taking it in turns to hold my hand, had now put some distance between me and them, and were giving me some odd looks.

Tod strode up to me, looking remarkably at home in that unfamiliar, mountainous environment,

"God, Fo," he said, "why're you walking like that?"

"Like what?" I asked.

"You look like one of the undead," he said kindly.

We both fell about laughing. I didn't doubt he was right!

Some time later the heavens opened and, right on cue dusk

became darkness. We'd been walking, and scrambling in places over the rough uneven ground, for well over an hour, and although Tod and I couldn't see it, we'd come to a small group of houses, the first habitations since leaving the village at the top of the mountain. This was the village of Lohrimani. Everyone piled under cover out of the rain, and, as is usual, Nepalese tea was quickly produced.

Lightening flashed brightly over the mountains, and thunder rolled through the valleys – all good, appropriate horror-movie stuff. The rain lashed down in an impenetrable curtain.

Amid much discussion our hosts had just about decided to put us all up there for the night, when an odd jangling and rumbling noise reached us from down the track. Here it came, the Nepalese equivalent of a knight in shining armour. A massive Indian-style painted truck, with rows of flashing red and blue lights across the front edged up to the houses, bouncing over the rocks, and squishing through the thick clay mud, its engine roaring.

The village of Salle is so isolated that few vehicles even try to reach it. Until recently there has been only a very small track to it, just about suitable for humans and animals. Now bulldozers have scraped out a wider track, but it is still only navigable by the largest of trucks, and even then it's touch and go. When the rains come the vehicles face the constant threat of becoming stuck in the thick mud. Even the new track cannot actually reach the village, and the closest the trucks can get is something like half a mile away. But here in front of us was a truck heading in the direction of Salle – what a bit of luck!

The children raced outside and, laughing and squealing, tumbled into the back of the truck.

Tod and I were pulled and propelled over to the cab by half a dozen over enthusiastic helpers, and through the ear splitting noise of the torrential rain hammering on the cab roof, one of them shouted to me,

"Your foot here," and he indicated a step on the side of the truck, roughly on a level with my chin.

I didn't want to be rude, and I wasn't sure if he'd understand, "You must be kidding," or, "No chance, mate!"

But in the remote Everest region of Nepal he who hesitates is simply launched head first into the truck cab.

I landed on the gear box cover thing, astride the gear stick, with my now soggy hat well down over my eyes, and my drenched garlands and scarves strangling me. Tod managed to climb in unaided, and now helped me into a more or less upright position.

There were already six people in the cab, including the driver, so I had to remain on the gear box as there was nowhere else to sit. With a shock I realised that what I'd thought in the dark was the back of the driver's seat, and so was leaning heavily on it, was in fact a man's leg. I apologised profusely to him, but no one spoke or understood English, and I hadn't yet mastered 'sorry' in Nepali. The cab's occupants all sat in complete and stony silence and stared curiously at me.

I had an idea that I perhaps wasn't giving the initial impression I'd hoped.

The truck's engine roared and we set off slowly along the steep, rocky, and now partially flooded track. The darkness was total outside the truck's headlights, and the rain formed an almost solid curtain. Visibility was practically nil.

With every bounce, jolt and bump I slid around on the smooth surface of the gear box cover, and even though Tod managed to get hold of my jacket collar, it was all he could do to hang on to me.

Adding insult to injury, the more the truck struggled to get up the steep track, the hotter the gearbox cover under me got.

I was tired, I was uncomfortably soaking wet and cold, and now this. I began to feel I'd just about had enough.

Suddenly the rain stopped, and I do mean suddenly. One

moment it was torrential, hammering on the cab roof, the next nothing. Smiles all round. But then within minutes, and with a sickening lurch, the truck sank half way up its huge wheels in soft clay. We were well and truly stuck.

The children piled out of the back, and with no more than a couple of small, weak-beamed torches between them to light their way, set off at a trot in a tight group towards the village. They were still laughing and talking, enjoying this adventure.

"Please don't let them throw me out of the cab," I whinged to Tod.

He had to yank me upright as the gear stick caught in my trouser bottoms, but luckily for me the truck had sunk so deep in the mud that I got out easily.

We set off after the children and I stumbled, slipped, and tripped in the dark on the unfamiliar surface. When we reached the end of the track we turned down the steep mountain side, following a narrow, slippy, rocky pathway. It was pitch black, and from the sounds all around we knew that everyone was scrambling rather than walking. But that knowledge didn't make me feel any better.

By this time I was so tired and aching that, predictably perhaps, I had begun to ask myself what I was doing there, in complete darkness, climbing down a steep, rocky path towards a remote Himalayan village.

At that moment I probably *did* look like one of the undead. I know I felt like one.

Somehow, an hour and a half later, we reached the village of Salle.

We were to stay at Dhan's parents' house. They were waiting to greet us, which they did in Nepali, and ushered us inside. This was our first experience of the inside of a village house. We sat on thin bamboo mats on the floor in front of the open fire, which provided the only light. As I looked round through the shadows, and my eyes became accustomed to the gloom, I could see that the room was absolutely packed with as many villagers as could squeeze in. They all wanted to look at us. They were all asking questions about us. Dhan was translating, as no one else spoke English.

A feeling of isolation crept up on me. How far away from home *were* we? How far had we walked to get to Salle? Would anyone in England ever find out if something happened to us here? How much longer could I stay awake?

To be honest, aching and tired as I was, I wished the floor would open up and swallow me. Just at that moment this did not seem like one of my better ideas.

One of the villagers ran out to find some forks for us to use, and we ate the meal which had been cooked for us on the open fire. It was delicious. Every bite was followed by the entire room. Tod tried not to dribble into his beard.

To everyone's delight Tod sampled the local raxi and pronounced it very good.

As I seemed to have solidified on the mat on the floor, I had to be pulled upright, much to everyone's amusement. And then finally we were shown our room upstairs, and were at last able to get some much-needed rest.

Our big adventure had begun.

Chapter Five

The first morning we woke up in the village of Salle was our first opportunity to see it in daylight.

The village bears no resemblance to an English village of course. It is in fact a collection of twenty-five or so houses, loosely grouped together, and built on terraces cut out of the mountain side.

There is no central road or track in the village, but rather a series of steep rocky paths between houses. Here and there two or three houses sit together, but usually they are in their own space, on their own terrace.

It could take you thirty minutes to walk to any particular house. I say 'walk', but this village clings to the side of the Himalayas, high above the valley floor, so 'walk', especially in **my** case is probably not the right description.

There is forest above the village, and there are terraces below it, running down like a series of huge steps to the valley floor. There are no shops or businesses, and there is of course no industry. The villagers live off the land, farming the terraces and growing to eat. They keep goats, water buffalo, cows, pigs and chickens.

The houses are built of brick, clay and wood, and Tod and I thought some of them looked something like Swiss chalets. They all have outside wooden verandas, upstairs and down, and the roofs are made of corrugated tin or slate. They look good, and fit into the environment well.

However, inside the houses they are what **we** would consider to be almost entirely 'empty'. There are no tables or chairs, no wall units containing TV and music making equipment, no kitchens or bathrooms, no computers, no washing machines, no fridges, no carpets, no heating other than an open fire, and no water other than that which is fetched from the stream…. In fact they contain nothing to which we in the West have become accustomed, and which we feel makes our lives comfortable and 'civilised'.

The open fire, which all the village houses have, is usually roughly in the middle of the floor downstairs. It is of course used for cooking, heating and light. Ventilation as such is non-existent, and the eye watering and choking build up of smoke in the room has to escape through the door or windows. Glass is more than a rarity, and all the windows we saw were simply small wooden 'doors'. Even in the daytime the rooms are very dark, and you often have to scrabble around to find the bamboo mat to sit on. The floors are simply solid clay.

The cooking 'utensils', metal plates and bowls, are usually stored at one side of the room, often on a series of wooden benches or shelves. Most houses have a rudimentary bed in the downstairs room, and an open wooden staircase leads to the upper room or rooms, which are used for sleeping. In these upper rooms you will find roughly made beds, but not a mattress in sight! And maybe if someone in the family is a good wood worker there will be a kind of cupboard for storage. As the villagers possess very few clothes, they do not need wardrobes or cupboards.

We realised early on that most of the village women seemed to have just two sets of clothes. They all wear either a kind of sari wrapped around the body several times, or a long loose top, with baggy trousers beneath; or sometimes a combination of the two. These are their every day clothes, worn equally when working on the crops, or when doing work in the village.

If they wear shoes at all, and most of them don't, they are open plastic sandals.

It is tradition for the women to wear large gold earrings and nose rings, and brightly coloured bangles.

It is fair to say that I stood out a mile as I wandered round the village, for numerous reasons!

The older men wear an odd kind of baggy trousers, with a tunic type top over them. I say 'older men', because the younger men tend to wear jeans and t-shirts most of the time.

However, we noticed that there were very few young men in the village. They have mostly moved away to find work, and some have gone abroad, leaving the wives and children to carry on the life of the village.

The village of Salle is proud to have electricity, and there are huge poles carrying the supply over the mountain and down the terraces into the village. But the electricity, when the supply is available, provides one light bulb per house, and little more. Few villagers bother to install or use electric lighting.

Some of the villagers now have a new device for cooking. This is a metal pot, with a small internal electric fan to blow air through the wood fire which is made in the pot. If the electricity goes off while they are using it they simply tip the burning wood into the open fire, and carry on.

The only water supply to the village is a fifteen-or twenty-minute walk away, down a very steep, rocky path. There is one small pipe, which provides water for drinking, washing and cooking. All the water you need, and your wet, washed clothes, have to be carried back up the steep, slippery mountain path. We had brought plastic water container bags with us, so we would clamber down to the water pipe, quarter fill one bag, and share the carrying of it back up the steep path. Initially, we made the mistake of washing quite a few clothes at the water pipe, and then discovered that the effort of carrying them back up the path was just too much for us. Soggy clothes are surprisingly heavy, and of course we were struggling with the debilitating effects of altitude too.

We found that whenever we did anything even slightly strenuous, breathing became difficult, and we puffed and panted and wheezed a lot of the time. We had to do everything slowly and carefully, and hoped it wasn't going to take too long to acclimatize.

Our room was upstairs in Dhan's parents' house, reached by a wooden staircase on the outside of the building. We climbed the stairs and went through a trapdoor onto the upper veranda. Then we climbed through a window – it had no glass in it, and was closed by wooden shutters – into Dhan's room. (Dhan lives in Kathmandu, and so was rarely at his parents' home.) Our room was off Dhan's room, separated from it by a sliding door.

We were privileged guests. We had two beds, a table, a chair, and a cupboard in our room. Did I mention that there were no mattresses? Huumm. My Gran used to say that sleeping on a hard bed was good for you. *Why on earth did she think that?* And, more to the point, I'd put money on her never having slept on a lumpy wooden board.

There were of course no washing facilities. It was a bowl of cold water outside, which was actually quite refreshing first thing in the morning, splashing cold water over your face and arms. Of course we had to be careful not to get the water in our eyes or mouths. And hair washing was great – I'd recommend a bucket of cold water anytime. Very stimulating.

The toilet was a three-or four-minute walk from the house, not counting negotiating the sliding door, window, trapdoor, and stairs. Bit of forward planning necessary there at night. And of course, although the toilet was inside a wooden shed, it was in fact just a hole in the ground with a couple of foot plates either side. Still, we found we were rarely alone in the loo, there was usually a nosey spider, and sometimes a snake in there too.

On that first morning Tod and I came out onto the veranda at about 6am and just stood looking across the valley. 'Breathtaking' didn't begin to touch it. On the other side of the valley was another mountain range, and behind that, when mists permitted, you could see the snow-covered tops of the Everest mountain range not far away. The mountains which are not snow-capped are forested right to their summits. We stared mesmerised across at the other side of the valley, at the countless terraces with their different crops, running down to a hidden river on the valley floor.

A group of massive eagles floated way out over the valley; we could hear them calling, and the noise of crickets and the chatter of birds reached us from all sides. Way below us someone was walking a group of water buffalo through the trees, and the occasional call from them floated up to us on the still air. Nice voices, water buffalo.

Most houses have a flat area of compacted clay in front of them. On that first morning ours was a hive of activity. There were hens with chicks and noisy cockerels everywhere; there were two mother goats with their kids, and a dog lying flat out in the shade, snoring.

Already, on that first day, we had our 'audience' of local children. This was to become habitual, and I cannot remember a single day when we did not have at least half a dozen children outside the house, morning and evening, no matter what the weather. They would sit on the hard clay ground and stare at us, even if we were only reading on the veranda. They found us fascinating!

They would chat away to us, practicing their English, and we had some great games with them, chasing around on the flat ground outside the house. The children would sometimes sing for us, or show us dances they had learned at school.

They were wonderful, bright and funny, untouched by the trappings of our 'modern' life. No computer games or chat rooms for them, no television or DVDs, no shopping, cinemas, parties.... The children of the Himalayas have to make their own entertainment, and they spend almost every waking moment outdoors.

We had to get used to being constantly followed around and stared at, by children and adults alike. The majority of them had never seen real live white people, and of course Tod was an endless source of amazement and amusement for them. He played well to the crowd, and they loved him and his beard.

The women would stand round and stare at me as I washed

my hair or brushed my teeth. They would touch my skin, comparing it to their own. All the women in the village had long hair, and they couldn't understand why mine was short. They'd pull at it as if they expected it to fall out.

Almost no one in the village spoke English, and most of the communication we had with the villagers was carried out via gestures, mimes and smiles!

Whenever we walked past, work would stop on the terraces, and people would come out of their houses to stare at us. Even the animals stared.

But there was not a shred of ill will against us. We greeted everyone with 'Namaste', and said '"Bye bye"' and waved when we left them. The village as a whole took this to heart, and soon everyone, everywhere, was waving to us and calling 'bye bye'. They liked the sound of 'bye bye' so much that the villagers would use it as a greeting, as well as a farewell. We loved it.

We always gave the traditional Nepalese greeting of 'Namaste', along with hands held together in front of the face. Tod started shaking hands with people we met, and this caught on too. Very soon everyone was doing it.

On our first day in the village Dhan took us to the schools where I was to teach. We went first to the state Secondary school, which is partly funded by donations from the UK.

It was not in the village. It was at the end of a forty-five-minute scramble down a very steep path. I was half dead by the time we got there, and of course panicked by the thought of doing the reverse journey, regularly, after a day's teaching.

We were accompanied by a retinue of nearly fifty children and adults that day, as it was a national holiday. There was great communal oohing and aahing, head-shaking and sharp intakes of breath each time I slipped and landed on my poor bruised bum.

I did eventually get there though, and after looking at the nine small classrooms, I had a look through the teaching resources and saw what I'd expected to see – a couple of dog-eared Jane Austen, some Thomas Hardy, several poetry books, and a shelf of English grammar books written by Indian professors. There were also some dictionaries and a few atlases which had all seen better days.

Maybe not the best material for small, eager children wanting to learn up-to-date, conversational English. Each classroom had a blackboard and chalk. There was no electricity or water supply in the school.

We then processed on to the Junior school. Kalyani, a lovely, bright girl who speaks good English was its young headmistress. She showed us the way. It was back up the mountain, but luckily for me it was only about a twenty-minute scramble.

The Junior school was called a Boarding school, which it wasn't. It consisted of two, one-story wooden buildings within which there was a total of five classrooms. It was set in the middle of a large flat area surrounded by forest and spectacular mountains (of course). When we eventually got there Tod and I just stood and stared around in awe, and our retinue did the same. Surely there never was a more magnificent setting for a school.

Then suddenly the children poured out of the classrooms and got into neat lines, with their teachers at the front. Although it was a holiday they'd all put their uniforms on and turned out to meet us – again. Most of the children have a thirty-minute walk, some as much as an hour or even more, to get to school. But here they were, on a school holiday too, putting on a show especially for us.

Chairs were produced and we were gestured into them. The children filed past us, some only two years old, the oldest thirteen. We were presented with flower garlands and scarves again, and the children sang some songs in English.

We both felt quite emotional.

Dhan made a long speech, which had the audience of children, teachers and parents laughing. He apparently said that because *we* seemed to be smiling all the time (he'd obviously mistaken my 'give me some air in my lungs' grimace) he wanted everyone in the village to smile at *us* all the time... .Huummm.

From the outset we received nothing but kindness and consideration from the villagers. We were well aware that they found us strange and hard to comprehend. We knew that we were an endless source of amusement and fascination to them. Doubtless they thought that we came from a far away country where all men have long beards and are comedians, and the women fall over all the time.

They accepted with a smile the fact that we didn't speak Nepali, and they laughed kindly at our futile attempts to do so.

They were forever inviting us into their homes for tea or a meal. They would even try to drag us into their houses for a cup of raxi when we were walking to school in the mornings! And yes, on more than one occasion we arrived in the classroom smelling of the local firewater!

They didn't even mind if we forgot to take our boots off when entering a house – mind you, the smell of sweaty trekking socks may well have played a part there.

And they didn't mind that neither of us could manage to sit cross-legged on the floor; we usually sat with our legs stretched out in front of us. It was all I could do to actually get down to the floor, and getting back up again was always a cause of much polite laughter. Did I say that I do 'undignified' really well?

Dhan gave the responsibility of looking after us to Kalyani, the Junior school Headmistress. She was twenty, and a human dynamo. She ran the school and had also begun a literacy outreach adult education programme, finding teachers to go out to remote homes to teach the adults to read and write.

Luckily for us Kalyani not only spoke pretty good English, but she had a wicked sense of humour too. We became very close during our time in the village. She took the looking after us bit very seriously. Dhan had told her not to let us out of her sight, which we found strange. It simply didn't cross our minds that there could be any danger to ourselves in that remote area, where everyone seemed so friendly.

However, there *were* locks and padlocks on everything – a padlock on the trapdoor, one on the glassless 'window', and even one on our sliding door. The wooden window 'doors' all had internal locks on them.

Eventually we asked about all this security, and didn't get much of an answer, certainly not a straight one. But when Dhan said he was leaving the village to go back to Kathmandu, and wanted us to promise him that we would never open the trapdoor or window after dark, *even* if someone called out to us, and we would always remember to lock up, and tell Kalyani everything we wanted to do so she could accompany us, we said, "*Why?*"

Again, we didn't get a straight answer, and certainly nothing that made any sense to us.

Later on Kalyani told us that Dhan rang her from Kathmandu nearly every day to check that she was looking after us.... So, there was obviously some unspecified, potential danger to us..... But we were almost never alone anyway, and we didn't feel threatened at all. We spent little or no time worrying about our safety.

When we arrived in the village the crops had just been planted, and most of the terraces were full and already worked. So there was nothing for Tod to do in the fields. There was also no village project underway which he could help with, such as building or water provision. So he came to the school with me, and took to it like a yak to snow.

The children loved Tod. He was always doing something to make them laugh, and of course they were absolutely fascinated by his beard. Wherever he went he trailed happily squealing children behind him.

It took me an hour each way to walk to and from the Boarding school. However, it took me an hour and a half just to get back home from the Secondary school, scrambling up that steep, rocky path, and I had to stop half a dozen times along the way to gasp and wipe the sweat from my face.

I knew it wasn't going to be realistic for me to teach there, and actually Kalyani, ever tactful, suggested that because the Secondary school had a lot of holidays, (it was a state school), it would be better if I just taught at the Boarding school, which didn't have so many. So that is what we did.

Yippee.

Chapter Six

At the time of the first famous chronicled attempts to conquer Everest, or Sagarmatha as it is known in Nepali, the settlement of Jiri, as I have already mentioned, was Everest's Base Camp.

It no longer is, but it *is* still a thriving, though very small town.

We were anxious to see where such famous names as Mallory and Edmund Hillary had started their ascents from, and we looked forward eagerly to our weekend in Jiri.

Of course Kalyani would not hear of our travelling there alone, so she booked bus tickets for the three of us. As a result of our somewhat persistent questioning, she had eventually told us that it was not safe for us to walk through the local forests alone because there had been a series of 'incidents' recently. These incidents seemed to have been attacks by 'strangers' on local people.

She also added something that sounded like *"and the tigers"* but I thought I hadn't heard her right, and as Tod made no comment, this was never further discussed.

But anyway, standing firmly between me and a weekend anywhere at all was the fact that I would have to climb up a mountain in order to reach the road and take a bus. This of course was the reverse trip from the one which we had made in the dark and rain, when we had first come to the village. My big worry was whether I'd actually manage the ascent, and make it all the way back up to the 'Village at the Top of the Mountain' as we then called it.

Jiri is only twelve kilometres along the road from The Village at the Top of the Mountain, but the thought of having to take a Local Bus even that short distance filled us with dread.

"Not to worry," I told myself, "What can happen in twelve kilometres?"

The working week is six days in Nepal (Saturday is the one day off) so we felt a bit guilty taking most of the Friday afternoon off too. We slunk quietly out of the village.

It was hot as we began the steep ascent towards the mountain tops, barely glimpsed far above us in the mist. I was puffing and panting, grasping outcrops and roots to pull myself up, aided by both Tod and Kalyani's nifty little shoves to my posterior here and there at appropriate moments.

We reached the village of Lohrimani, and walked through it along its only road, and out the other side in ten minutes, politely resisting all invitations from half a dozen of Kalyani's relations to take tea or raxi with them. They stared anxiously after us as we headed for the mountains.

Then the really hard part of the ascent began – the climb through the rhododendron forest to the top of the mountain. The red rhododendron is the national flower of Nepal, and the rhododendrons which grow in that country bear little resemblance to the dainty ones to be found in the UK. In Nepal the rhododendron is much more of a tree than a bush, with large gnarled trunk, and thick, solid branches.

There can be few more spectacular sights than a rhododendron forest in flower in Nepal, covering the side of a mountain. However, I dare say that not many of us have ever had to climb through one!

It took us nearly three hours to do so, due mainly to my wheezing and panting, tripping and sliding, and much loud questioning of my sanity.

"If you ever suggest doing anything like this again it's an immediate *no*!" I snapped at Tod. Odd, isn't it, how in times of stress we tend to forget who instigated the stressful situation!

Tod just smiled. He didn't even seem to be sweating, whereas my arms looked like mosaic patterning where the sweat running down had cut paths through the thick coating of red dust over them. I could just imagine what my face looked like at that moment....

Somehow we reached the Village at the Top of the Mountain, and Kalyani led us to the area where the buses stop. My legs were wobbly with the strain of the climb, and I flopped down on the wooden veranda of a small store to wait. It was just before three o'clock.

But the three o'clock bus never came. The first thought, shared by the villagers and ourselves, was that it had slipped over the edge of the mountain somewhere along the way. We never found out what had happened to the three o'clock bus.

So we waited, the three of us squashed together on the small wooden veranda.

Our habitual audience grew from seven chickens and a pushy cockerel to eight small children and half a dozen adults, mainly women.

I noticed that the accustomed friendliness of Salle village seemed to be lacking here at the top of the mountain, and some of the faces even seemed to be scowling in our direction.

The people were not as clean in body and clothing either, even though we were sitting no more than five yards from a communal water pump. I felt slightly, unaccountably apprehensive, and it occurred to me that I would not like to have been waiting there without Kalyani watching over us.

Some time later Kalyani introduced us to a young man with a friendly smile who called himself BJ. He spoke good English.

"I have a guest house in Jiri," he told us, "You're welcome to stay there."

Things were looking up. BJ and Kalyani disappeared off to have tea together.

Then it began to rain, and rain, and rain. It fell as only, I presume, Himalayan pre-monsoon rain can – straight down, in massive heavy drops, forming an almost impenetrable curtain. Tod and I squished back as far as we could on the veranda, away from the muddy, bouncing spray, and I watched the hens run for cover, followed by children and adults. Himalayan hens seem to have extraordinary long, stocky legs, topped by feathers that look suspiciously like running shorts. I wondered if this was why, as I watched them leaping over the puddles that had already formed along the main street, and leading the race for cover. Fascinating.

The noise of the rain pelting down was ear splitting on the tin roofs, but we had nothing else to do so we sat and watched the dust turn to mud, and the mud begin to slide off down the road along which we still hoped our bus would come.

Just before six o'clock and the rain had not let up at all, a tiny bedraggled boy ran up to Kalyani and told her a bus was coming. This news spread quickly through the thankful little group of by now weary potential travellers. There were about ten of us waiting for the bus to Jiri.

We heard it coming before we saw it, even above the all-pervading crashing of the rain, as it laboured up the hill. Round the bend and into sight it came, steam fizzing off the hot engine cover, moving at no more than ten mph up the steep hill towards us.

We quickly gathered our backpacks – we'd brought small ones that could go in the bus with us – pulled our hoods over our heads, and stepped out into the downpour.

It felt remarkably warm as we trotted across the road to the get on side, and gathered there in a small, expectant group. I looked down the road at the approaching bus and noted the bright blue tarpaulin covering the luggage on the bus roof. And then, with much creaking and screeching, the massive Local Bus drew to a stop next to us.

For a split second an oasis of quiet calm descended on the scene, even the noise of the rain seemed hushed, and we all breathed in ready to step onboard.

Then all hell broke out.

With loud and heavy screeching and jerking movements the bus door drew back in an attempted concertina movement, but the sudden screaming which accompanied this pointed to the possibility that someone inside was squashed in said movement.

At the same time the bright blue tarpaulin on top of the bus rose several feet into the air, depositing massive dollops of hitherto trapped rainwater onto us, and the twenty or twenty-five people who had been travelling on the bus roof (cheapest seats) jumped, climbed, slithered, and in one case fell down from the roof, and attempted to enter the bus through any available opening.

I heard Kalyani yelling,

"Fiona! Get on the bus!"

I was standing behind two Nepalese men who were attempting to do just that, with no success, and although I was head and shoulders above them I couldn't even see the bus steps.

There were thrashing arms and legs everywhere. People were shouting at the tops of their voices.

Kalyani was still yelling, but in Nepali now, and she suddenly appeared at my side, grabbed my backpack out of my hands, and launched herself at the two hapless Nepalese men in front of me.

Small she may be, but made of steel she certainly is, and under her onslaught they moved forwards and up onto the bus steps.

The bottom step now hove into view in front of me, and Kalyani grabbed my arm and yanked me up onto it.

As I swayed there, momentarily off balance, a brown leg swathed in voluminous pink cotton shot over my shoulder and into the bus. I couldn't believe my eyes! Had that really just happened? A young woman had swung down from the roof and entered the bus over my head.

Right-oh.

The bus driver, for reasons best known to himself, chose this moment to move the bus forward several feet, sprinkling assorted Nepalese along the road behind him.

I was still on the bottom step, just, and now I shouted to Kalyani above the bedlam,

"I can't do this! I can't get on," and I tried to get off. But she was having none of it and shoved me hard from behind,

"There won't be another bus," she shouted, "get on!"

The two men in front of me were wedged and immobile, shoulder to shoulder across the entrance, the only gap between them was at about my chest height. They, like everyone else, were shouting, adding to the uproar. Suddenly, from within the bus, a hand shot through the only gap, and a voice shouted,

"Fiona, come through, there's room inside."

It was BJ. Kalyani gave me another shove, and I instinctively grabbed the proffered hand.

Before you could yell 'sports bra' I was through that gap and nose to nose with BJ. I craned round to see what was happening behind me just as the bus began to move forward again. Through the open door, over the ongoing struggle, I saw Tod and Kalyani and my backpack still outside.

"Tod!" I yelled frantically, "Don't leave me on this bloody bus!" and I saw them both begin to run to keep up. Then I was pushed back into the aisle of the bus and lost sight of them.

"Here," BJ said to me, "Step over here and stand in the middle."

The combined weight of a great many damp Nepalese pressing into me was too much for me to remain where I was, but of course 'step over' was something I'd long since forgotten how to do there in Nepal, so I fell over the habitually floor-dwelling bag of animal feed, and joined it on the floor in the middle of the bus.

By the time I managed to pull myself up into a semi-standing slouch, by hanging on to the back of a rusty seat, the bus was well under way, and I was sure I was on my own in it. But Tod's voice,

"Fo, where are you?" reached me, although I couldn't see him. Thank God he was there.

Somehow I got myself upright and stood hanging on with

both hands to the ceiling rails running overhead. I could see Tod now and Kalyani with him. They must have been the last ones on; they were standing on the steps. I wondered how they'd avoided the door when it closed, and began worrying already about what they'd do when it opened again.

By now the bus had reached maximum speed – twenty mph or thereabouts – and was snaking upwards along what passed for a road, bumping and swaying as it went. I struggled to stay upright – no change there – and smiled thankfully at Tod and Kalyani.

Kalyani had been worried about me.

"Are you ok, Fiona? I'll get you a seat shall I?" she called over.

"Oh my God, *NO*," I thought in horror, imagining just what kind of a scrap would develop if she started clearing damp Nepalese off the seats, and I was sure she was capable of it.

"No no, thank you, I'm fine, Kalyani," I said hastily, "Absolutely no problem," and I put on my best 'We're British. We can handle this, it's nothing at all' facial expression.

"Are you feeling ok?" Tod called over. Obviously my expression needed some perfecting. "Pass your backpack over here and I'll look after it. You might not fall over it then when we get off!"

Twenty minutes of swaying, screeching round bends, and bumping through potholes later and a loud yelling, whistling and banging on the side of the bus heralded the first stop.

Instead of trying to squeeze along to either the front or back door, those Nepalese travellers who wanted to get out, and who found themselves sandwiched, exited through the open windows.

We started off again.

I could still only see ahead and slightly to my left. The press hadn't relaxed enough to allow me to see down the sheer drop side, so I contented myself with watching the mountain pass by two inches away outside the window.

The sheer drop, on the other side, was indeed a very sheer drop. Tod, Kalyani and I had struggled up the mountain from the village, and we were still going up. I bet Edmund Hillary never took a Local Bus, I thought.

The rain continued to absolutely hammer down. We made two more noisy stops in short succession, seemingly in the middle of nowhere. I wondered how far those people who got off would have to walk. They weren't exactly dressed for this weather – some of them didn't have shoes on, and those that did only had plastic slip-on sandals. None of them had waterproofs. They either had umbrellas, or plastic bags cut along one side to fit over the head -– this was the preferred method of keeping dry up there in the mountains. I looked down at my waterproof jacket....

Suddenly there was a huge bellow from the back, loud whistling, and banging on the side of the bus, much louder than before. Everyone in the front jumped, and I saw Tod lean across and look out the bus window towards the sheer drop. The bus didn't stop, and the shouting and banging continued. Tod moved back, picked up my backpack, checked it quickly, and dropped it by his feet. Then he looked over at me, and I remember thinking what a strange look he had on his face.

When we got to Jiri the bus stopped right outside BJ's guest house, and we trotted in and got a room. All the rooms had mountain names on the doors, but we'd never heard of ours. BJ assured us it was part of the Everest range, and we realised how limited our knowledge of those mountains was.

Later on Tod said to me,

"I don't care if we have to walk back, but we are definitely not getting on another Local Bus."

He told me that when the loud shouting and banging had happened in the bus, and he looked out the window, he realised that the bus had moved slightly towards the edge of the road, to avoid a recent landslide that had reduced part of the route to rubble.

But the bus's back wheels couldn't maintain their grip in all the mud and debris, and they had actually begun to slide off the edge of the mountain.

Obviously the people at the back of the bus had seen and felt this, and panic had ensued.

Tod then checked my backpack to make sure our passports were there so our identities would be known if and when the bus was ever recovered from the valley floor far below.

We had a great dinner that evening. There was a wonderful atmosphere of celebration everywhere as the next day was Nepalese New Year 2066. Yes, *2066*. The Hindu calendar is used in Nepal. It is a lunar-solar system, fifty-seven years ahead of our Gregorian calendar.

Although it was exciting seeing Jiri, and knowing how much history has been made there, I have to say that it is not the most attractive of places. There is really only one street, which is not too clean, and oddly enough although you are on top of one, you can't see any other mountains. We call it a 'town' because our Nepalese friends describe it as such, but Jiri is really only the size of a large village.

After dinner the next day we sat and chatted with Kalyani. We had already grown very fond of her, and were impressed with the way she coped at such a young age with a heavy and varied workload. The villagers seemed to look up to her, and she was forever sorting problems out for them. She, like the others, found us strange, and she always had a hundred different questions to ask us about our lives in England. We spent a lot of time laughing with Kalyani.

That evening we taught her how to sing '*Old MacDonald had a farm*'. She particularly liked the sound of the '*here a woof, there a woof*' refrain, and we had to sing it with her over and over again! Even after we'd all retired for the night we could still hear her, in the next room, '*woof woofing*' quietly to herself.

We left the guest house at 6.30am the next day, to get the bus back to the Village at the Top of the Mountain. But even before we'd started to walk along to the bus park – to get a mini bus rather than a Local Bus – we knew something was wrong. It turned out that the buses were on strike.

We have never yet fully understood the reasons for the strike, but we do know that two motorcyclists ran head first into a Local Bus on the road just outside Jiri the previous day, and were both killed.

Tod and I sat down at the edge of the road while Kalyani went off to see if anyone could give us a lift back. She returned shortly with a young man who was driving a small, open backed truck.

Knowing by then that nothing ever happens quickly in Nepal, Tod and I remained sitting and listened while the talking began.

Some time later Kalyani said,

"Come on, get in. He's going to drop us off."

Gratefully we clambered into the back of the truck with our rucksacks and a couple of hundred books we'd bought for the school. There was just enough room to sit on the floor.

We set off, but stopped again almost immediately, so that another six people could cram themselves in with us. We all stood. We may now hold the world record for the greatest number of people and books in the back of a small pick-up truck, in Nepal. We were squashed, and pretty uncomfortable, but it was a beautiful sunny morning, and the drive back was really pretty – part of the way took us through Jiri forest – and we actually felt safer than if we'd been on a Local Bus.

It was fun.

A group of local women working outside a house spotted Tod as we drove past and yelled

"Welcome Ali Baba!" and we all laughed and waved back.

In no time at all we were belting out verses of 'Old MacDonald', with special emphasis, of course, on the *'woof woof'* refrain.

Chapter Seven

During the initial two-week trek most of our group had developed coughs and sore throats, some really quite bad. This is unfortunately one of the prices to be paid for venturing above what our bodies consider to be a sensible altitude.

Tod and I counted ourselves lucky that we held out until the end of the second week, before succumbing to altitude coughs.

Obviously we'd all suffered the inevitable stomach upsets from time to time, but a trekker's best friend is his Imodium....

Once back in Kathmandu after the trek we realised that the whole world there seemed to be snuffling and coughing, but given the prevailing conditions – appalling air quality, and the searing heat sending clouds of filthy dust into the already polluted air – that didn't seem odd.

Tod and I had just finished our first course of antibiotics, brought with us from the UK, when we arrived at the village, and for a couple of days we were cough and wheeze free. But then the coughs came back with a vengeance, accompanied by sniffles and chest infections.

We carried on, trying not to let ourselves be restricted by health concerns.

However, we were very aware in the village of the lack of oxygen in the air. It is weird to take a deep breath and feel your lungs telling you that it is not enough, and demanding more. There is roughly twenty percent less oxygen in the air up in the village than at sea level, and the higher you go, the less oxygen there is.

Everywhere I went I puffed, panted, and gasped for air, and had to force my constantly shaky legs to keep on going. Tod fared rather better than me, but for *him* to feel breathless after simply walking up seven steps to our veranda, is strange and worrying.

In a way we got used to it, and tried to adapt, learning to do everything slowly, even brushing our teeth much more slowly than usual!

However, our bodies have not evolved for a life much above sea level, and just as the Yak cannot survive much below 3,000 metres, we have to 'acclimatise' to survive at high altitude.

After finishing my third course of antibiotics, with no noticeable impact on my wheezes or cough, and Tod coughing too, although less, we decided we would have to leave the village and descend to a lower altitude for a while.

This is how mountain climbers acclimatise, and it is the only real way to tackle the problem.

We'd both become a cause for concern in the village, and there seemed to be a sense almost of communal guilt around, because of the detrimental effect the altitude was having on us. The villagers told us our ailments were the result of prolonged exposure to the altitude, and the climate. Although it seemed to us a bit odd that the climate could bear much responsibility for our ailments, we did acknowledge that the frequent changing from very hot, to windy, to rainy, to chilly and back again, sometimes all within an hour, probably did play a part.

Anyway, try as we might we could not shake off our ills, and although we hadn't allowed them to stop us joining in village life, we were now aware that the villagers were worried about us. They knew when we'd been coughing in the night, and they noticed if we struggled more than usual getting to and from school, or going down to do the laundry.

We had to go. Kalyani booked us a mini bus from the Village at the Top of the Mountain back to Kathmandu for a period of rest and recuperation.

I was dreading the climb. It took me a long, long time to get up the mountain again and through the rhododendron forest. Tod and Kalyani were great, taking it in turns to push and pull me over the steepest parts, and we spent quite a lot of time giggling like kids.

We had decided to stay overnight in the Village at the Top of the Mountain because the bus to Kathmandu leaves from there at 7.30am.

I have to say that the village would make a good, ready made film set for a 'Hammer House of Horror' film. It actually bears a great resemblance to the 'Village of the Damned'. It is dark, and the darkness of the village has only a bit to do with the unwashed people and dirty streets – there is something else there. I don't think I ever saw an inhabitant smile – plenty of scowls, but no smiles. From the moment we reached it that day it became known to Tod and me as *The Village of the Damned*.

We stayed in a boarding house there overnight. The only spare room had three beds in it, so we all shared.

The beds had no mattresses, which was usual. We slept on boards with a piece of thin material draped over them. To cover you most places provide what appears to be an old blanket filled with tatty, irregular shaped sponge pieces; it is usually not too clean, and usually has no cover on it.

We all chose our beds and Tod and I sat on ours while Kalyani disappeared off to try to find something for us to eat.

A short time later the door swung open without a knock, and one of the leading actors from The Village of the Damned strode in.

The woman, who was probably about fifty, was above average height for a Nepalese woman. Her long dark hair was scraped tightly back from her face, emphasising its features, which were strong and grim. Her clothes, hands and face were grimy. Her unexpected presence seemed to fill the small room.

We were taken aback, and just sat stock still on our beds and stared at her. She glared back at us in silence. Then she walked to each bed, checked it, although we didn't know what she was looking for, and then without a backward glance, she left the room.

We dissolved into giggles (how old are we?) and spent the

next ten minutes speculating on the reasons for her visit, each reason wilder than the last.

Then suddenly she was back again, this time carrying a pile of bedding.

We stared wide-eyed at her as she headed purposefully towards Tod.

I swear he cringed as she arrived in front of him, and tossed the bedding at him. Then, just as the first time, she turned and left the room. The door slammed shut after her. Not a word had been spoken.

I started to laugh and laugh. It wasn't so much the fact that Aunty Fester had singled Tod out for special beneficial treatment that tickled me, but the fact that she'd given him a pillow and an eiderdown both covered in beautiful, clean, pink material.

"Love the floral designs," I said, "Very fetching!"

I was still giggling when Kalyani came back, and of course that set me off again. We took the mickey out of Tod all evening, but he didn't care. He said he was very comfortable in his pink bedding, and didn't offer to swap with either of us.

The next morning, following a night which Tod and I spent coughing and wheezing, pink covers or no pink covers, we were up and waiting for the bus in plenty of time.

It was only an hour late, and when it came we settled into our seats for the eight-or nine-hour journey.

Of course we knew it'd be a long and tiring day. You count yourself lucky if your posterior remains in touch with the seat for as long as ten minutes, and reading is impossible. When I tried that I spent more time retrieving my book from behind the back of the person in front of me.

So off we set in the ten-seater mini bus, Kalyani in the front, and Tod and I together just in front of the back seat.

There was a young Nepalese couple sitting behind us on the back seat, and they had a baby with them of no more than six months. For the first hour or so the baby, incredibly, given the swaying and jolting of the bus, slept peacefully on its mother's lap.

But then she woke up, and unsurprisingly began to cry. The power of the noise that can be emitted from such a small pair of lungs always amazes me.

The parents played with her, trying to keep her amused and stem the flow of piercing screams. I suggested to Tod that maybe she was crying because she didn't like the loud Nepalese music that as usual filled the small bus. Any conversation has to be carried on in raised voices in order to be heard over the music. This journey was no exception.

So over the next few hours we bumped, crashed and swerved through the startlingly beautiful scenery of the Himalayas, deafened in turn by the screaming of the baby, the soothing (!) noises from the parents, and the outrageous belting out of popular Nepalese music. No chance of nodding off.

Some time later Tod said,

"They've got a cat toy for the baby."

"How do you mean?" I said, "I've never seen any kind of toy here."

"Listen." Tod told me, "It's a toy that makes a meowing noise."

And sure enough, over the chaotic jumble of noises in the bus I could just make out a small meowing noise from behind us.

The baby, now on her father's lap, had quietened down.

"That's a real cat," I said.

"No, it'll be a toy," Tod said.

But you see very few children's toys in Nepal, let alone one which would require the mechanism to make a cat noise. However, there are also very few real cats in Nepal at the moment; we had been told that a disease had practically wiped them out a few years ago. So far we had seen only one cat in the village. So both possible explanations for the noise behind us seemed unlikely.

More out of boredom than anything else, we both turned and looked back through the gap between our seats. The young couple smiled at us.

"Have you got a cat toy?" Tod asked them, loudly enough to be heard over the assorted noises around us.

"Yes, yes," the young man said eagerly, nodding and smiling. We could still hear the meowing.

"Look! Look here!" he said, plonking the baby none too gently into his wife's arms, and reaching down towards his feet. The baby screamed loudly, indignant at being plonked anywhere.

The young man sat back up again, clutching a Hessian sack in his hands, a huge grin on his face. We stared at the sack, and the first glimmers of comprehension began to dawn.

Then everything happened really fast.

The young husband grabbed the sack's drawstring, pulled it, and the sack fell open. A small, spitting fur ball shot furiously out of the sack.

The husband instinctively threw his head back, away from the onslaught, leaving his throat a clear, unprotected target. Before you could yell 'jugular' the tiny kitten had fastened pointy teeth and razor sharp claws into the unfortunate man's throat, and was clinging there growling.

His wife screamed in fright and dropped the baby onto her knees – it of course screamed even louder. We didn't understand what the man was shouting, but we presumed it was along the lines of,

"Get this small kitten off me please"

His wife, and a passenger on the other side of her husband started frantically trying to disconnect the fur ball, which continued to growl, from the man's throat.

Tod and I glanced at each other, wide eyed and open-mouthed, and quickly turned back towards the front.

No one forward of us seemed to have any idea what was

happening on the back seat – there were too many other noises going on in the bus.

I had little sympathy for the man, and a great deal of sympathy for the small, undoubtedly hungry, thirsty, and terrified little kitten. After a few moments the kafuffle on the back seat subsided, but we didn't look back, we didn't want to see the inevitable results of this short-lived escape attempt.

The young couple got off the bus shortly after – we were nearing Kathmandu – and I noted with some satisfaction that he was dabbing at his bloodied neck.

The Hessian sack and its unfortunate occupant went with them.

We spent a week recuperating in Kathmandu, trying to get rid of our coughs, and then returned to the village feeling better, but not completely cured.

Chapter Eight

Dogs in Nepal are a bit of a problem for me. By that I mean the way they are treated. I have never understood cruelty to animals (or humans, for that matter) in any guise, and I looked on in horror there as children and adults alike would walk past a sleeping dog and hit it with a stick.

Why?

To me it was totally unnatural to see a puppy too afraid of humans to come over and play with you, and an adult dog cringe away, rather than accept a well-meaning stroke.

The dogs live outside of course, and there seemed to be one or two of them for each house or cluster of houses. Sometimes they are thrown scraps, sometimes not. Unfortunately for them, they inhabit that dim nether land, somewhere between wild and domestic, and have ended up with the worst of both worlds.

Nepalese dogs have a job to do, as does every living thing that struggles to survive high up in the mountains of the Everest region. They guard the other animals, and the houses. But they are not appreciated, and they are certainly not loved.

'Woolly Head' as Tod christened him, the large black and brown dog who lived outside our house, was probably no different from any other Nepalese canine. As we got to know him his character revealed itself. He was a bumbling, gentle giant. His face was a picture the first time I offered him a biscuit. He saw it in my hand, and having surely never been hand fed by any human, he literally didn't know what to do. So, standing a couple of feet away from me, he just opened his mouth in hope. I moved nearer and popped the biscuit in between the pearly white gnashers. Woolly didn't really seem to believe this miracle until he had munched and swallowed.

Now, whether this was a good move on my part, a bad move, a thoughtless move, a natural action.... I have still not yet decided.

Wasn't it that great man Gandhi who said,

"The greatness of a nation, and its moral progress, can be judged by the way its animals are treated"?

Maybe so. But this statement seems to me to beg a hundred further questions, and how on earth do you discuss something like this without seeming to, or actually making judgements?

But my belief is that Woolly Head and his ilk are miles above us lowly humans, and I frequently found myself thinking how much the Nepalese people were missing out on by denying themselves the love of a good dog; and of course they are not alone throughout the world.

Instead of seeing a gang of laughing, shouting children running through the forest with a couple of excited, barking dogs in their midst, there in the valley we saw the gang of children, but the dogs were running away from them, usually amongst a hail of stones thrown at them by the children.

From time to time, in the intense, silent dark night, we heard Woolly and some of his colleagues start barking – an eerie sound, echoing up and down the valley, and off the mountain sides in the dark.

We could usually tell the degree of seriousness Woolly attributed to the intruder by the intensity of barkiness.

It was usually,

"I can hear you, and if you come any closer I'll get you. I'm warning you, I have teeth and I know how to use them."

The intruder's route was marked by the trail of barking down the valley in its wake.

One night, in the dark silent early hours, Woolly started barking with a hitherto unheard intensity. Tod and I were instantly wide awake and hardly breathing as we listened.

Woolly's angry snarling and furious barking was augmented by his colleague's at the house directly below us – he was also giving it everything he had.

And then another bark joined in alongside Woolly's, but this one was unfamiliar, quieter, and slightly less aggressive. I suddenly realised that it was the slender, dark-furred, glamorous piece from over the hill at the back, next to Kalyani's house.

Well well, she must be over here on a late night assignation with Woolly, the sly old dog.

He sounded anything but sly or old as we listened to him pounding up and down on the hard clay at the front of the house, checking the perimeters.

This time it was definitely,

"I can hear you, and when I spot you I'll tear you apart!"

Although we were inside, and probably quite safe, it was a pretty frightening thing, just listening to the dogs securing their territories.

Not a single plonker opened a window and shouted,

"Shut that bloody dog up," or, "We're trying to get some sleep here!"

The only sound in the valley was the Fur Brigade doing its job. Everyone knows they are the first, and probably the only line of defence, so no one interferes with the Fur Brigade in full cry.

Little by little the intensity dropped and the noise abated. The valley began to quieten down. Woolly stopped racing round, and we could hear him huffing, puffing and grumbling to himself. Eventually even the small growls ceased, and the valley fell silent again.

I wanted to rush outside and shake him warmly by the paw,

"Well done, old boy. You have single pawedly saved this house, and all who sail in her, from certain death in the jaws of a marauding wild tiger. God bless you, my boy."

Never a truer word said in jest.

Of course, it may not have been a tiger. It could have been a Yeti. Funny things, Yeti. I kept hoping we'd see one, but apparently they live at much higher altitudes, so the only ones we might have seen would have been the bad map readers.

I mentioned the existence of the Yeti to several Nepalese, citing Edmund Hillary's statement that he saw a Yeti footprint on Everest. Oddly enough, they all smiled in the same gentle way, and told me that Edmund Hillary was a really good friend to Nepal. It took me a month to work that one out.

We started to have a bit of a problem with Woolly when he took to following us to school. The path to the school passed right in front of several houses, and three of those houses had canines who took their positions very seriously.

The first time Woolly followed us we simply thought he'd get bored, and go home, and it really didn't occur to us that we'd meet any major problems along the way. Anyway, we couldn't persuade him to leave us, so we carried on.

After a bit of a snarling disagreement, and some canine name-calling at the first house, we were nervous about Woolly's prospects at the next two houses.

And well we should have been, because here the first dog, having the advantage of sunning himself on an upper terrace, had spotted us coming. He must have done a bit of nifty semaphore to his buddy as well, because the moment the top dog launched himself out of the blue onto poor old Woolly, it turned into a two-pronged attack, with the other dog appearing from below the path and joining in.

The shock was quite stunning for Tod, myself and Kalyani, so for our Woolly it must have been dreadful, and he disappeared under the two snarling black dogs.

The noise of the fight, and us shouting, brought the couple running out of the house.

Usually Nepalese people will simply stand and watch an animal fight, often laughing and enjoying it. But we were having none of it, and as we threw sticks and whatever we could find to separate the dogs, Kalyani shouted to the couple who were standing nearby, to help. They did. And very fast. They seemed embarrassed that their dog had attacked Woolly – by now everyone in the village knew that Woolly was our friend.

A subdued Woolly came and lent against my legs. No harm done this time. Only wounded pride. Believe it or not, Woolly was not a fighter.

He trailed us into the school, and spent the morning mooching round, keeping an eye on things. The children avoided him. When Tod went off back along the path through the forest to top up our water bottles before the lunch break, Woolly went too.

Some time later Kalyani and I were sitting together on the wooden bench outside the school house, watching the children enjoying playtime. It was a very hot day. We'd just given the kids a couple of yellow tennis balls, and a game of catch and chase had developed.

Suddenly, almost as one, the children stopped their game and turned to look up at the path where it comes out of the forest, and drops down into the school ground. There was a swell of murmuring and oohing and aahing, and a couple of the children pointed up towards the path.

"Hey, look at that," I said to Kalyani, "All we need now is the music from 'Raiders of the Lost Ark.'"

Tod and Woolly had emerged from the forest. Man and dog were perfectly in step, and you couldn't have fitted a piece of paper between them. Tod had his Raiders of the Lost Ark hat on, and a couple of water bottles slung over his shoulder. His blue, mirror style sunglasses caught the sun and glinted.

They advanced together down the path into the school ground, and the children stepped back and cleared the way for them. You could have heard a pin drop.

"I think I should be making some comment about dramatic entrances, and limelight," I said. Kalyani and I were giggling.

Of course any similarities to a popular film were entirely lost on Tod's young Nepalese audience. None of the children had ever been to a cinema, or even watched a DVD.

But they were mesmerised by man and dog, the pair of them in step and walking so closely together. The children had never seen this kind of human/canine interaction before. Without the 'benefit' of TV or internet in the village, they had no stick to measure against.

Getting Woolly back home, even accompanied by Indiana Jones, looked like being quite a problem. However, the children had it all in hand, and as a group of about fifteen of us traipsed back along the forest path at the end of the school day, they sent runners ahead, requesting that the 'problem' dogs be tied up before Woolly arrived.

When we reached the second and third houses all was quiet as we approached them from the back (except, that is, if you ignored the loud, anxious beating of my heart) and followed the path round to the front.

Tod, Kalyani and I smothered laughter as we saw, on the flat clay at the front of the house, the little boy who lived there standing perfectly still, his hands over the eyes of his large black dog, who was also standing perfectly still.

We all tiptoed past, Tod with his hand on Woolly's scruff, warning him to behave. No one said a word. The black dog's tail wagged.

Once round the next corner of the path we all breathed a sigh of relief.

"I'm never doing this again," I said, "My nerves won't stand it."

No sooner were those words out of my mouth than the black dog came hurtling round the corner after us. The little boy must have let him off too soon, and the dog, realising he'd been duped was out for revenge.

"*Run!*" we all shouted, and with Woolly leading the way, we all broke into a gallop along the high, narrow, and in places crumbling path which followed the very edge of the terrace.

We must have run for four or five minutes, but it seemed like an age. When we stopped I could hardly breathe, even Tod was panting, and we were all sweating in the hot sun. We looked back along the path, hoping to see that the dog had given up the chase and gone home. But there on the path, not far behind us, child and dog were in a bundle – each had the other in a headlock, and the child's giggles, and the dog's wagging tail were proof that it was a good game, as it should be.

Sadly, this was the only time in all our months there that we saw playful canine/human interaction, or in fact anything other than human aggression against dogs in Nepal.

Chapter Nine

Throughout the month of May the hot, dry weather in the village gave way little by little to rain-soaked days, and very chilly mornings and evenings.

Knowing my tendency to spend quite a bit of time slipping and landing on my posterior even in dry weather, Kalyani began suggesting that on the days of heaviest rain, we didn't attempt to navigate the path to school. We had already seen the damage done by last year's monsoon waters, and marvelled at the power it must have taken to completely remove large sections of the path.

Even before we came to the village it had been decided that we would leave it during the month of June, so as to avoid the worst of the monsoon rains, and we were hoping to be able to visit Tibet at that time.

By the last week of May both Tod and I were ready to leave the village for a couple of weeks, for a number of different reasons.

Obviously, the advent of the monsoon was the prime reason, but we were also suffering the unexpected effects of a much restricted diet.

The villagers live on a diet of rice with a kind of curried or spiced lentil sauce called 'Dal Baht'. They eat only two meals a day, breakfast and an evening meal, and both meals consist of rice. Apart from the rice they eat boiled potatoes, and very little else. During the day we sometimes saw the children eating home made 'popcorn', and occasionally mango.

Practically no fresh greens were available in the village; very little fresh fruit, (although the villagers do collect *wild* berries and fruit in season, they do not cultivate it themselves), and no cheese. I asked about the cheese, I wondered why it wasn't made in the village from maybe goats', buffalos' or cows' milk. The answer seemed to be that no one knew how to make cheese. That knowledge appeared to have been forgotten over the years.

Kalyani brought us eggs from another village, buffalo milk, and was sometimes able to get bananas for us, although by the time they reached us they were usually going black and, to our Western eyes, were therefore very unappetising.

I am vegetarian, but Tod was offered meat on three occasions during our stay – once chicken, once pork, and just before we left for good the villagers slaughtered a water buffalo and shared the meat amongst everyone in the village. But this happens only very rarely. Meat really doesn't form a part of their diet. However, fresh fruit and vegetables also do not form a regular part of the village diet. This surprised us as the villagers put their hearts and souls into the cultivation of potatoes, corn and millet, and the crops appeared (to our untrained eyes) to do very well. But although the villagers *do* eat the potatoes, the corn goes to feed the chickens and other animals, and the millet is only used to make raxi.

Vegetables and fruit are not specifically cultivated, and apart from some vigorous varieties of squash, which reseeded themselves annually, we did not see any other vegetables growing around the village.

Even the rice has to be brought in from other areas as Salle is too high to grow it successfully there.

So for the first month Tod lived on the packets of trekking food we had brought with us (he is not keen on rice at the best of times), and I ate Dal Baht. To start with I enjoyed it, but I have to say that there is only a certain amount of rice I can happily and enthusiastically eat, and after a month of two almost identical rice meals a day, and no greens, I started to find it really hard going.

Throughout that time we ate at Kalyani's, and she prepared our meals on the open fire in her house. It was usually dark outside as she cooked for us, and the only light in the house was provided by the open fire. But as the weather deteriorated

Kalyani insisted that we eat in our room, and she began bringing our meals to us, saving us from having to climb over the hill to get to her house, where we often arrived like a pair of wet rats.

Consequences followed from this decision.... Left alone in our room with our meals we usually had several candles burning on the table, and often laughed about the 'romance' of candle-lit dinners in that far-flung place! However, with the benefit of light upon the subject we could now actually *see* what we were eating. Those small black lumps which I had thought were spices in the sauce, were actually flies....

I sorted through each individual grain of rice in the following three or four meals, extracting the bodies. There was an almost complete flying cockroach in one meal, but the 'end' came for me when after the usual sift I thought I was safe, and so stabbed with a fork at what I assumed was a larger than average grain of rice. The prongs bounced off, and even on a second attempt didn't penetrate the object. A few seconds of short-sighted scrutiny told me this was no grain of rice – it was a maggot.

The discovery that I had been dining on rice and a variety of insect life for the past month coincided with the end of Tod's supply of trekking food. Rice was off the menu for both of us now, but we had few remaining options on the table. We needed a plan of action.... Tod decided to show Kalyani how to make chips, and *I* promised not to ask where the cooking oil came from.

So, for the rest of our time in the village we lived on chips and hard-boiled eggs.

Perfectly acceptable.

However, we eventually found ourselves craving the food our bodies were lacking. We started to have dreams about food, (how weird was that!) and spent a very rewarding hour one evening making a list of what we'd have to eat the day we got back home to the UK. Our stomachs rumbled constantly. We had both lost quite a lot of weight, although this was probably due in equal parts to continual hard physical exercise and to lack of food.

Many years ago Tod injured his back, and from time to time it reminds him of this. Considering all the physical exercise we'd been having since arriving in Nepal, it was therefore not surprising that his back chose this moment to complain again. He began to limp, and he struggled to climb the path to school. The hour journey began to take us much longer.

It was time to return to Kathmandu.

Kalyani, small but super strong, had once likened herself to an 'ant', and the name had stuck. In fact we often called her our Pack Ant, especially when she pinched whatever we were carrying and carried it herself. She hated to see us carrying anything.

But even for our Pack Ant, carrying two rucksacks up the mountain (Tod's back problem would not allow him to carry his rucksack) to the Village of the Damned was out of the question.

So we cut to a minimum everything we intended to take with us, and ended up with one small, reasonably light backpack, and one full-sized, medium heavy backpack.

"I'll carry the big backpack," I said, and Tod laughed.

"Even when you were carrying the small pack it pulled you over backwards and you ended up on your bum again," he said.

He can be so hurtful.

On the Saturday we were due to leave the village Kalyani bounced into our room in a state of excitement.

"Guess what!" she called, as she leapt in through the window.

"We're so lucky! My uncle says the truck that makes the deliveries to the nearest village can now get further along the track. And the driver will stop above our village and pick us up!"

Kalyani holds the world record for possessing the greatest number of aunts, uncles, cousins, nephews and nieces, so we felt it prudent not to ask her which uncle she was talking about. We'd made that mistake before, and had never managed to follow her explanations.

"Oh wow!" we said, "and where'll he take us? How far?"

"All the way up the mountain to the top," she said, dancing around and pulling Tod's beard. It had become a sort of ritual, this beard pulling. Most people did it, and Tod just grinned.

The track the truck would take us along went round the mountain and upwards, ending up in the Village of the Damned at the top of the mountain – just where we needed to go. It wasn't always navigable for the whole distance, but apparently just at that moment it was. We were in luck.

We set off to climb up to the track, far above and behind the village. It was only a half-hour ascent, but very steep. I made it with the large rucksack on my back, which probably said a lot about my increasing level of fitness, but I was very glad to sit down beside the dusty track to wait for our lift.

We waited and waited. We sang a couple of verses of 'Old MacDonald', doing the animal sounds in English and Nepali. Amazing how similar they are. You wouldn't know the difference between a British cow and a Nepali cow.

Eventually the driver rang on Kalyani's mobile to say he was delayed.

So we waited some more, and admired the view of the valley from our vantage point.

A young man from the village joined us. We waited.

Then, with engine coughing, and tyres throwing out thick clouds of dust off the track, a different truck rolled unsteadily round the corner towards us. This one was a massive open-backed affair, with a chunky cab, in which two men and the driver were sitting staring at us. Kalyani leapt to her feet, pulled open the passenger door, and started talking very fast and very loudly at the men.

Their expressions slipped from interested astonishment, to glazed, in no more than thirty seconds.

"Come on," she called to us, helping (pulling, actually) one of the men down from the cab, "I've said your back's ill, Tod, and

I've said…."" she looked at me doubtfully, "I've said you're old, Fiona, so they'll sit in the back and you two can sit in the front and be comfortable."

"No, no," said Tod, "We're fine in the back."

"Yes," I agreed with him. God knows why, not one of my better decisions, "We'll be fine in the back."

And Tod was up and over the tail-fin thing in no time, bad back or no bad back, and chucking our backpacks into a corner of the completely empty truck.

I looked at the back of the truck, and at the massive tyres, and I wondered if altitude makes you lose your grip on sanity.

Poor Kalyani was hopping around loudly begging Tod and me to reconsider our undoubtedly ill-considered decision.

"Do you know," I called up to the happily grinning Tod, "I think it probably does affect your judgement."

But just at that moment he looked like something out of the 'Boys' own Own Annual' circa 1955, and I knew he was having a great time. Oh dear.

I started the ascent of the tail thing, but it went badly. The bit of my brain that deals with commands to the feet seemed to be malfunctioning over there.

As my beloved was now doing impressions of *'Ships, I see no ships'* it was left to the very nice young man to help me up and into the back of the truck to join Nelson.

Kalyani was beside herself, and had reverted to shouting at us in Nepalese. We got her drift. The nice young man helped her into the truck too, and muttering darkly she wedged herself into a vacant corner.

"The view's great," I said. She ignored me.

Three or four Nepali ladies suddenly appeared and threw pretty flowers into the back of the truck to us. I wondered if they knew something I didn't. Was this goodbye? We saw the oldest lady in the village hurrying along, bringing flowers for us, but she was too far away, and we could only shout our thanks to her.

The truck's engine roared, we waved to the ladies who stood together watching us, and then we were off along what I instantly realised should not be called a track at all, but rather just a collection of potholes, rocks and rubble, vaguely connected together, like a jigsaw done by a child.

The sides of the truck were about three-foot high, and the ridge on top of the sides was sharp, making hanging on even more difficult.

We lurched along at no more than ten mph, every so often tipping over dangerously close to the edge of the track, which of course ran along the very edge of the mountain. Progress was rough, to say the least, and hanging on was not easy, necessitating a kind of crumpled posture and constantly cricked neck. Doubtless I resembled an anxious garden gnome.

Tod was in his element. He was having fun.

The view was amazing – we could see all the way down to the very bottom of the valley, terrace after terrace, and all the way up to the top of the local mountain range. The air was even clear enough to see the next, snow-capped range, home to the mighty Everest.

We came to the first bend and things did not go well there. The truck nearly lost at least one of its occupants.

Kalyani yelled at me,

"Fiona! Your feet are not staying on the ground!"

Yes, that was true. But as long as my hands stayed attached to the truck's side, my feet could do their own thing – they usually did anyway. I grinned at her.

Kalyani shouted again,

"I think this is a strange kind of transport for an English teacher!"

I did too. We laughed. I felt like a naughty kid. It was great.

We arrived in Lorhimani, a collection of twenty or so wooden houses strung along what even by Everest region standards was a rough track, and drove bumpily through it in state, waving to a selection of Kalyani's aunts, uncles, and cousins who all came out to look, wave, and marvel at what we were up to now. I tried my best to look relaxed as I held on for dear life.

One of Kalyani's little nephews was just starting to walk up the mountain, and she shouted to him to climb up into the truck and we'd give him a lift. The little lad joined us and stood holding on next to Kalyani.

We reached the end of the road through the village and turned sharply right, to begin the steep ascent of the next mountain. We were all tipped backwards and then sideways like milk bottles in a crate, and clouds of sandy dust blew all over us.

Kalyani began to laugh, and Tod and I turned and saw her little nephew with a thin, spiky conifer branch sticking out of his ear. He'd forgotten to duck, and the conifer had whacked him on the head. Kalyani couldn't help herself; she was crying with laughter. It took quite a while to retrieve all the needles, and the poor kid must have been very uncomfortable. He looked miserable and embarrassed.

The truck began to really labour up the steep track, and we had to keep stopping for various kinds of Himalayan traffic jams: oxen; goats; water buffalo – when you get a chance have a look into a water buffalo's eyes – absolutely wonderful face, huge eyes, sweetly vacant expression, tendency to dribble. What a creature.

The last part of the ascent was spectacular. We circled the rhododendron forest, swaying, crashing into potholes, and swerving on the thick dust. In places you'd have thought the truck was going to tip over backwards the ascent was so steep, and we hung on grimly, trying to avoid slithering uncontrollably to the back of the truck.

But we made it, and the truck stopped on the main street of the Village of the Damned just as the rain started to pelt down. Right on cue.

We climbed out and asked Kalyani how much we should pay

the driver.

"I'll handle it," she said, and immediately entered into what sounded curiously like an argument with one of the men. We stood shuffling our feet and awaiting the outcome.

After a few moments the man got back into the truck and slammed the door, then shouted something through the window in our direction. Kalyani calmly trotted to the back of the truck and made a note of the number plate. Something seemed to have gone a bit wrong with the transaction, we thought, but Kalyani was giggling.

"Do you know," she said, "He wanted double because you are foreign. So I asked him if you weighed more than the average Nepalese, or if you took up more room than one. He was a bit rude."

The poor man, I thought, someone should have told him that he hadn't a hope of winning an argument with our Ant.

The truck drove off, and we ran for cover from the rain.

As the last time, we stayed overnight in the boarding house, and guess what? Yes, Tod got preferential treatment again, and ended up with a pretty pink pillow case, and a white bedcover with pink flowers on it....

A pattern seemed to be developing.

We were up and out early the next morning. Kalyani wasn't coming back to Kathmandu with us, but insisted on seeing us safely onto the bus. While we waited I watched the hens. They fascinated me. Kalyani couldn't understand why I wanted a photo of a Himalayan hen, but nevertheless she helped me chase around after one until I got a half-decent photo, runners' legs and all.

When the mini bus arrived it was full, even though we'd already paid for our seats on it. Unfortunately this is normal in Nepal. The bus drivers squash in as many people, animals, bags of grain, sacks of potatoes, and drunken Nepali men as possible, regardless of who's paid or reserved what.

But they didn't expect us to have a Nepali Ant with us, and in no time at all Kalyani had cleared out the two women who were sitting in our seats, and told the driver where to drop us off in Kathmandu. Yet again we were grateful for her help.

We settled in, and waved goodbye to Kalyani, ready for what should be the usual eight-or nine-hour journey.

Apart from the mind-altering music – and here words fail me – it was quite a pleasant drive for the first six hours. That is, if you leave aside the bumping, jolting, swerving, screeching to an inexplicable stop, and crashing and skidding through running water on the road…….. to mention but a few of the usual accompaniments of a journey through the Everest region of Nepal.

We were looking down on the heavy monsoon clouds most of the time, and the scene was spectacular. The mountain tops, most of them snow-covered, reached out of the swirling clouds, and we could hear crackling and booming thunder from time to time. The rain stopped, and we were able to see quite a distance when the clouds parted.

The crops were obviously much more advanced than the last time we'd made that journey. Now the terraces were full, and the landscape appeared quite dramatically altered.

After about six hours we began to notice trucks parked at the side of the road, and groups of people walking along the road in both directions. The route started to become congested, and eventually we could go no further through the press of vehicles, people and animals.

We pulled in and stopped. There were no vehicles coming along the road towards us, only people, so we assumed there must be a strike and a blockade set up by the villagers in the next village, preventing vehicles passing through.

These strikes were quite common in the Everest region at that moment. If the villagers had a grievance with local or central government, they simply blocked the road and cut off public access through their village, until some notice was taken of their problem. Ninety nine percent of the time there was no other possible route around the village, unless you left your vehicle and climbed the mountains, so massive inconvenience was caused, and notice would most certainly be taken.

However, we had not seen any anger displayed by the long suffering Nepali public, only understanding and acceptance of these situations.

Tod and I didn't bother to ask anyone what the problem was, we just assumed the road would be opened again in a couple of hours, so we settled down to wait.

It was very hot. The narrow road on which we were parked was rather like a sun trap at that point. We watched the streams of people walking past leading animals and carrying all manner of things – beds; live chickens; bags of grain; and elderly people – yes, we often saw sick or elderly people carried on someone's back. Almost two hours went by.

We were travelling in the bus that day with a group of young Nepali nurses and their boyfriends. We didn't know them, but we had been chatting with them for a while. They wanted to know if Tod's beard was real, and if all English men had beards. Our laughter was interrupted by one of their group who had been for a reconnaissance walk along the road. The news was bad. We would have to leave the bus and walk, he told us, because there had been a landslide and the road could not be cleared.

This was a shock. I felt something akin to panic. How far would I have to carry the large backpack? I wasn't sure I could manage a yard in that heat, let alone a mile or more.

We got out of the bus, with poor Tod hobbling and obviously in pain, and picked up our packs. One of the men travelling with us on the bus who'd been acting as driver's mate said,

"We just have to find the driver and he'll take us back to Kathmandu from the other side of the landslide."

Hang on, we thought, a couple of questions spring immediately to mind here – where *is* the driver (he'd left the bus at least an hour ago), and just *how* will he be able to get us back to Kathmandu from the other side of the landslide?

But answers came there none, so I struggled into the large backpack, and we started walking, following the little group from our bus.

The narrow road was absolutely crowded with what looked remarkably like an exodus of refugees from some disaster. We had to push past people, frightened goats, and overflowing handcarts, all seemingly determined to get in our way.

We were both sweating by the time we had walked downhill and onto the village street. I could hardly breathe, and my sunglasses had steamed up, making the one-foot-in-front-of-the-other bit even harder.

And then we saw it. Just the other side of the tiny village the narrow road runs between a small but fast flowing river on one side, and a sheer mountain face on the other. But the road was now completely blocked by huge boulders, some of which had rolled off the road and into the river, while others still hung precariously on the edge of the mountain face, looking as if they could topple down onto the road at any moment.

There was no other way. We had to climb over the boulders to reach the other side of the landslide, where we could see a line of buses collecting people who had done just that.

Right-oh.

There was quite a jolly atmosphere as we struggled over the boulders. Everyone just seemed to take this hold up in their stride, and even *I* made it across without too many stumbles.

As soon as we reached 'dry land' Tod and I shrugged off our backpacks and sat down on them, panting and sweating.

"No, no," the driver's helper said, pointing at us, "We must find the driver. Don't sit down now."

If I'd had more breath available to me at that moment, I know without a shadow of a doubt that I'd have said something polite like,

"If you don't mind we'll just sit here for a little moment to catch our breath."

But in the absence of enough breath I just glared sweatily at him.

"Come on," Tod said, "Let's get this over."

So we staggered to our feet, and got the packs on again.

"Why do we have to find the driver?" I asked the driver's helper, "Can't we just get on one of these buses – they're all going back to Kathmandu?"

"He'll take us," was the answer. I found that unsatisfactory.

"But he hasn't got a bus now," I was getting peeved, "so why don't we get on one of these?"

We were standing in full view of a line of about fifteen assorted buses, all going back to Kathmandu, and all filling up rapidly with those who had been similarly dispossessed of their original means of transport.

But he scurried off followed by the other members of our group and, much against my will we followed too. Ten minutes later we'd walked past every waiting bus, and there was still no sign of our missing driver. I was absolutely shattered and in no mood to continue the search.

"Come on," I said to Tod, "We're getting on one of those buses, and if that plonker tells us not to I'll chin him."

Tod agreed, and we turned and walked, well staggered actually, back along the road.

"This one's pretty empty," Tod said, indicating what at first glance looked just like a long lump of rust and broken glass, with a wheel here and there.

It was a Local Bus, but needs must; I felt I couldn't take another step. My hair was plastered to my forehead, and my glasses were still steamed up. Great.

We took off our backpacks and walked to the bus's external ladder, meaning to pass our packs up to the bus roof. But all the space on top was already taken, and two goats were standing on the roof, ready to make the journey too. We'd seen many goats travelling dangerously up on bus roofs, and the plucky chaps never seemed to sit or lie down, preferring to stand and go with the flow, leaning into corners, their hair blowing out in the slipstream around them. I always worried about them, but Tod told me that they wear special rubber hoof suckers for these journeys, so they're pretty safe.

Being unable to offload our packs, we had to lift them up the bus steps and inside with us. I heaved and strained, and eventually manoeuvred my backpack up onto the bus floor in front of me. There were plenty of free seats at the back, so using both hands I managed to lift the pack in front of me about three inches off the ground. Waddling like an elderly duck, I set off down the centre aisle.

Ten seconds later I was flat on my face on top of the backpack.

I hadn't been able to see the floor in front of me, and so had missed the fact that it was full of sacks of potatoes. Tod, behind me, grabbed my t-shirt none too gently, and pulled me to my feet. I swear I heard him say, "Not again," but he denied it.

"Just go and sit down," he said, "I'll bring the rucksack".

Seriously though, have you ever tried to walk over sacks of potatoes? It should be made a sport at the Olympic Games. 'Potato Walking'. I'd lay money on Nepal winning Gold.

There were no ceiling hand rails, so I hung on to the backs of seats in my unsteady, hunched over progress along the aisle. Of course the Nepalese are much shorter and generally smaller than us Westerners, so given the additional height of a sack of potatoes, my head was more than brushing the bus ceiling. Doubtless I looked like Quasimodo on a particularly bad day.

I reached the pair of seats just in front of the back seat, and was relieved to see a thick metal pole running floor to ceiling beside the narrow entrance. I grabbed it, meaning to use it to swing myself round into the safety of the seat. But the pole simply came free from the bottom, and thumped me in the chest.

I had to scrabble quickly with feet and hands to stop myself falling again.

You know, I find Nepal a really tiring country.

When Tod joined me in the seats he reassured me that I wasn't responsible for the free-falling pole. It had never been attached at floor level, and you could see the road below through the hole. Humm.

Following loud and well-meaning suggestions from several passengers, Tod had put our large rucksack on the seat behind us, the back seat, next to the window. That seat had rapidly filled up, and I wondered now if we should drag the rucksack off it to allow another person to sit there. I turned to look back and assess the seating situation behind us.

To my horror, the statutory drunk Nepali man, who'd been practically carried onto the bus, now had an arm around our backpack, and was holding it close, whispering sweet nothings into its top flap.

"*No!*" I shouted, standing up as best I could in the very restricted space, and twisting round "*No!*" and I tried to bat the man away from the pack, but couldn't reach him.

"He's going to be sick over it," I shouted to Tod, "*Do* something!"

Tod looked round and located the drunken man's friend, who was also sitting on the back seat, although seemingly not drunk himself. Whatever Tod said to him, in a quiet voice, had him out of his seat in a flash, and pulling his drunken friend off our backpack and away to the other side of the back seat, where he attempted to get the drunken man to go to sleep.

But for the rest of the journey I worried about our backpack, and kept turning round to check that it hadn't become the object of the drunken man's affections again.

It was 7.30pm and dark by the time we reached central Kathmandu. We'd been held up by a political demonstration that blocked the road past the airport, and then we'd tried several petrol stations until we found one with some petrol in it. We were tired and aching, and longing to sit down on a seat that didn't bounce around all the time.

"Shouldn't be long now," Tod said, "We'll get a taxi to the hotel".

Shortly after that passengers started getting off at each stop, and we found ourselves alone on the bus, except for two young Nepali women.

Kathmandu seemed to crowd right up to the bus windows as we drove slowly through the centre. We had to drive slowly because there were people everywhere, not only on the massively over crowded pavements, but right across the roads too. Not for the first time I thought there just seemed to be too many people to fit into the city.

People browsed round the pavement stalls, or sat in groups on the sidewalks laughing and talking. There were cars, motorbikes, rickshaws, bicycles, pushcarts, and the occasional cow, everywhere.

When finally we got off the bus, stiff and tired from the journey, the two young women took pity on us and offered to show us the best place to get a taxi.

We followed them gratefully, and ploughed our way uncomfortably through the crowd milling around on the pavements for a good ten minutes.

We stopped at a large roundabout with a flyover stretched overhead, and stood at the side of a three-lane road. Each lane was clogged with all manner of vehicles, and the air was full of noise and dust. The women showed us where the taxis stopped, and kindly told us to take the first one in the queue.

The taxi driver told us he knew our hotel, so we agreed the fare without too much bargaining. We then realised how small the taxi was. We got in and had to put our rucksacks on our knees. But we didn't mind because the drive should only take ten or fifteen minutes, so we could cope. We started yawning in anticipation of a good night's sleep on a rock-hard bed.

The engine sprang into life, and we shot off along the road *backwards*.

The taxi driver, whose head was now within inches of ours, as he craned over to see out the back window, was tickled by our expressions of horror.

"No worry," he cackled, "I do this all the time. Only a fool would drive forwards here. Too much traffic. This is much quicker."

We looked at each other, speechless. I wondered whether it would be prudent, just at that moment, to point out that there seemed to be a fundamental misunderstanding here regarding the Highway Code. Mind you, *was* there a Highway Code here?

Our erratic backwards progress was followed by a swathe of hooting and shouting (we still hadn't learned any Nepalese swearwords, but now here was our chance), and then suddenly the driver swerved out across the lanes of traffic, still going backwards, towards the other side of the road.

"*Shit!*" we both said together, staring about, wide-eyed, at the traffic bearing down on us.

"No worry. Nearly there," the driver grinned. He seemed to be enjoying our fright. The engine was starting to make an odd screeching noise, and only dropped an octave when we braked sharply to avoid a wandering cow.

Kathmandu cows are either the world's most optimistic creatures; the world's bravest creatures; or they are missing a vital part of the brain. *Or* it could be that someone has told them that in the event of an altercation with a vehicle, *they* will never be to blame. The driver of any vehicle unfortunate enough to hit one of the wandering cows will indeed most probably face a term in prison.

We somehow reached the other side of several lanes of manic traffic, but instead now of joining the flow, we careered backwards round a slip road, straight into a waiting police van.

Well, well.

Do you know, it was perhaps a measure of the amount of tolerance that we had by then built up for 'strange' Nepalese ways, that the first thing I did was to look at my watch and say,

"I hope this won't take long." How cool was that?

The driver started muttering loudly and rooting through the doorless glove compartment. A series of unidentifiable and unmentionable things dropped out.

From our rather low position on the backseat of the small taxi, our view hindered by the rucksacks on our knees, and the fact that it was dark outside, we saw a pair of uniformed legs approach the driver's door.

The taxi driver at last found the papers he was looking for, and opened his window. He attempted to pass the papers out to the policeman, with no success. The policeman was having none of it.

"If I were him I'd get out of the car and start apologizing," Tod whispered to me.

But the driver obviously had no intention of doing that, and a heated exchange began through the open window. It went on and on, getting louder and louder.

"He's not going to win," Tod whispered, and I looked at my watch again.

We expected the driver to lose the argument, but we didn't expect another policeman to come over, open the car door, and drag the driver out.

Right-oh. We shrank back behind our rucksacks.

The driver's loud shouting decreased somewhat as the policemen dragged him towards the police van, and then it became muffled as they slammed the van door shut on him.

We looked at each other.

"How long shall we wait?" I asked.

"Give it ten minutes," Tod said.

Nine minutes later a very subdued driver flung himself back

into the driving seat, and slammed the door shut. Without a word he started off, and to our relief this time we went forwards. We didn't dare speak.

After a few minutes silent progress the driver turned round to us (yes, turned *round* to us) and explained that because he'd argued with the policeman he'd been arrested and fined. We nodded sympathetically, but fraudulently. What did he expect?

A short time later we knew we were lost when the driver stopped and asked a passer by for directions to our hotel. Oh joy.

Twenty minutes later we finally arrived at our destination, and listened open-mouthed as the driver told us we'd have to pay the fine for him, as it was *our* fault he'd been given it.

Certain choice words sprang to mind, but we declined to comment, and climbed silently out of the taxi. We did pay him more than the agreed fare, but not the fine.

Our rock-hard bed awaited.

Chapter Ten

Mention Tibet and most Western minds will conjure up the same mental pictures, starting perhaps with the alluring mysticism of that long-isolated country, but certainly followed closely by what we've all heard throughout the years following 1959, which saw the 'integration' of Tibet into China.

We share a general view of a country oppressed, of a religion suppressed.

I had long wanted to visit Tibet, but thought I'd never get the chance. When the border opened again during our stay in Nepal, I said to Tod,

"Let's go during our monsoon month off. We **must** see it. Tibet! What a chance! Wow!"

This was the opportunity we'd been hoping for.

He said, "Yes dear" or something similar. Sometimes he's not quite as enthusiastic as I am.

So, arrangements made, we left Kathmandu at 5.30am one very warm June morning, in a large 4x4 Jeep thing.

We were joined in the Jeep by a New Zealand couple, Sharon and Adrian, and we all got on really well from the start. They were funny, very well-travelled, and called a spade a spade – great companions as it turned out, for such a great adventure.

We were going to drive north, up to the Tibet – Nepal border, pick up a Tibetan guide on the other side, and continue in another 4x4 all the way to Lhasa, Tibet's capital city, a 5-day drive away from the border. We were due to spend 8 days in Tibet in all, and then fly back to Kathmandu on a Nepali Airlines flight. Guess what the Nepali Airline is called? Yes, *'Yeti Airways'*. Couldn't be anything else, could it?

"What an adventure," I squeaked. I can be such a child at times.

It took us about six hours to reach the Nepal-Tibet border,

and considering the nature of the Nepali roads, the drive was surprisingly incident free. When the border crossing eventually came into view, we were dismayed to see that it was literally surrounded by huge piles of stinking garbage.

Nepal has a *massive* problem of waste disposal, or rather, lack of waste disposal. Outside of the few major cities there is no organised waste collection, and no designated waste-disposal area in most villages. Even in 'our' school the children will simply drop rubbish at their feet, and walk away. They are not encouraged to dispose of rubbish carefully. Tod and I started 'The Great Rubbish Collection' hour, and once a week we had a competition to see which children could pick up the most rubbish. It was then dumped in a hole on the mountain side and burned.

On either side of many villages we saw waste tipped down the mountains in huge, stinking heaps, sometimes visible for miles around. The river which runs through the town of Jiri was completely choked with garbage. When the monsoon rains came, and the river level rose, this garbage was washed downstream en masse. We wondered where it finally ended up. We actually found the lack of awareness of this problem shocking, but everyone we spoke to about it told us that there was no money available for waste disposal programmes, and anyway it was simply not viewed as a problem.

As we got out of the Jeep at the Nepal-Tibet border crossing the smell, made worse by the heat, hit us all in the face. We wrestled our rucksacks away from a group of locals who wanted to carry them, and trotted fast towards the large metal gate, which was the exit from Nepal. Tod's troubles began there.

He was suddenly grabbed by three men and an armed guard, and pulled into a small hut, but thank heavens they only wanted to examine his tattoo more closely, and have a good look at his beard. They eventually released him with jovial handshakes all round, and cries of "Bye bye, Ali Baba!"

We walked across the bridge between the two countries. As we reached the Chinese (Tibetan) side, Adrian announced he was "wearing Free Tibet boxers, for support". We entered China roaring with laughter.

A mix up over guides, names on lists, and transport meant that the four of us had to wait outside the ultra-modern customs building until our Tibetan guide arrived to pick us up from the other side. We had no idea how long he would be. It was very hot. We piled our rucksacks up against a wall, and sat on the hot flagstones to wait. The scene around us was like something out of a sci-fi film. There were uniformed Chinese soldiers and armed border-guards everywhere. They were *all* wearing face masks, and we assumed they were conscious of the swine-flu threat. A very tall Chinese man – head and shoulders above the rest – wearing a long blue surgical gown with a white plastic apron over it, a face mask, an operating theatre cap and boots, and white plastic gloves, was wandering around peering into people's faces. He looked like a Chinese version of Beaker, from the Muppet Show.

A Chinese official approached us with a spray gun at the ready, and talking loudly and gesticulating, cornered us like bluebottles. He sprayed our rucksacks with what smelled suspiciously like Dettol, and they began to steam in the heat.

There was nowhere to get out of the sun.

Two hours later, and we were seriously wilting by now, Tod and I were summoned into the customs building. Our Tibetan guide was waiting on the other side of the checkpoints, and a young Chinese guide was going to take us through customs and introduce us to him.

We soon discovered that the Chinese guide didn't know the process. He escorted Tod and me up to the first desk, and we were immediately shouted at by the masked official on the other side. We interpreted his shouting and finger jabbing as, "Please go back and wait over there".

We did. Humm. Good start.

Five minutes later the official pointed to me and shouted something. Obediently I trotted up to the desk and proffered my passport. He snatched it up and slapped it down in front of his computer. Then he held the photo page open, and scrutinised me for a good thirty seconds.

"Go," he growled, pointing to the scanner machine with one hand, and slapping my passport back on the desk with the other.

P'raps a bit of customer-service training may be useful here, I thought, and I took my passport and walked over to the scanner. I heard Mr Charming shout again, and knew it was Tod's turn. I watched him walk up to the desk, passport in hand.

The female official at the scanner had obviously drunk from the same bad temper bottle as her colleague, and she snarled at me as I put my rucksack on the belt. It went through, and I picked it up again and looked round to see where Tod was up to. But he'd gone. Mr Charming was shouting at his next unfortunate victim, and Tod wasn't behind me at the scanner.

"Where's Tod?" I asked the guide, who was leaning on a vacant desk looking at his paperwork.

"Oh, he'll be around, don't you worry about him," the young man said, patting my arm.

The words 'patronise' and 'red rag' applied immediately, and although I'm naturally quite polite I said,

"Cut the crap. Just find out where Tod is, will you."

The young man shot off without another word, and I saw him yapping to Mr Charming. A couple of minutes later he was back.

"They have taken Tod to the Quarantine Room, to be examined" he told me, pointing to a room with 'No Entry' on the door. "We'll just have to wait."

"But why?" I asked, "Why are they examining him? There's nothing wrong with him."

"They think he may be sick like a pig," the young guide said.

I honestly don't think he was trying to be funny here, but I glared at him anyway, just in case, then I went over and stood waiting outside the examination-room door.

Twenty-five minutes later Tod emerged. Apparently the customs officials use special body heat seeking cameras to assess a person's temperature. However, we'd been sitting outside in thirty-degree sunshine, with no shade, for two hours before we went into the building, so it was probably not surprising that Tod appeared to have a high temperature.

He put his rucksack through the scanner and we walked together to the next desk. This was another passport check, manned by an even brusquer official than the first. Same process, same scrutiny, and then off to another scanner, this one for both baggage and person.

I went through, picked up my belongings and turned to check on Tod's progress. He was still standing at the passport check desk, and the official was waving Tod's passport around and jabbering at him. Tod still had his usual calm, friendly expression on his face, and he obviously wasn't understanding what the official was saying. Suddenly the official turned to the young guide, who was still hanging round, and said something to him.

"He says wait here," the guide translated, and the official, holding Tod's passport as if it had already bitten him, left the desk and walked out of the building.

Odd. We stood and waited.

Fifteen minutes later the official reappeared, slapped Tod's passport down in front of him, growled, and gestured to the waiting scanner. Tod and his passport went through with no problem, but before he could rejoin me, two uniformed officials appeared and told him to unpack his rucksack. They rummaged through the contents and pounced on a novel I'd been attempting to read. One of them picked it up, and with the other looking over his shoulder, started thumbing through it.

"Good luck, mate," I thought, "*I* couldn't understand it, so I don't know how *you're* going to."

Sure enough, a couple of minutes later, the official was asking Tod what kind of book it was, and what information it contained. I was summoned, and resisted the temptation to be sarcastic.

"It's a novel," I said, and the official chucked the book down and walked away.

We were finally free to leave the customs building. It felt as if we'd moved in, we'd been there so long.

Outside we met our Tibetan guide, whose name translated as 'Long Life', (how wonderful is that?) and the driver. Together with our New Zealand travelling companions, we climbed into another 4x4 Jeep, and set off on our journey to Lhasa.

The road from the border crossing went up and up. It was very narrow, with a sheer mountain face on one side, and a sheer drop on the other. It was in turn under construction and completed, but we had little or no warning of when we were about to change from one section to another, so we crashed over ramps, crashed down potholes, crashed through rubble, in short, we did an awful lot of crashing about.

We all held on tight and oohed and aahed at the incredible height we were driving at. We seemed to be *impossibly* high above the valleys and ravine floors, and every so often we veered or skidded uncomfortably close to the edge of the narrow road. Did I mention that the safety barrier hasn't made it to Tibet either yet? From time to time the route was almost blocked by boulders and scree, and we had to inch our way round the blockage, perilously close to that sheer drop. Tod loved every minute of it – the height, the views, the danger....

Our driver wasn't hanging about either, and when the road seemed clear he'd go for it, standing on the brakes when yet another large stone or boulder appeared in the road ahead. I began to wonder where all these stones had come from, and of course the simplest explanation was the right one – they'd fallen from the mountain above. Right-oh.

Long Life told us, with a smile, that this road was not passable during the rainy season, as there were too many landslides then. We looked at each other, and wondered when the rainy season was — it was *now*, wasn't it? But no one spoke. A feather of anxiety tickled the back of my neck.

Rounding a corner at quite a lick we almost ran straight into a massive boulder on the road. This one was truly huge. At first glance it looked as if we might not get past it, but our driver managed to squeeze the Jeep through the gap between the boulder and the edge of the road. We all avoided looking down. Once past the obstruction we saw, with a huge shock, that a car had hit it on the other side, and was now lying on its roof against the boulder.

We stopped, and all of us got out and ran to the car. Oddly enough, we had passed no more than two or three other cars on the road the whole day, but now another car arrived at the scene, and also stopped. But the crashed car was empty. We supposed the accident had happened a while ago, and the driver had been taken to safety, but we never found out for sure.

We carried on. Darkness fell, but our driver didn't seem to notice. He certainly didn't slow down. The landscape had changed as we drove through it. The trees and indeed most vegetation had all but disappeared. Now, in the Jeep's headlights our surroundings looked seriously spooky, as if we had entered another dimension. We drove on and on.

Finally, we reached a village. Well, Long Life said it was a village, but I had my doubts. A few habitations straggled out along one road.

The place seemed more like a depository for huge piles of rubbish and rubble, although we couldn't see the details too clearly in the dark, which was probably an advantage.

The 'hotel' was ramshackle, we didn't need much light to see that, but we were all so tired that it didn't matter, we were just glad to stop for the night.

Construction work was still going on along the road, and

certain stretches of it were closed at various times during the day. We had to leave very early the next morning so we could get through before any closures. So we were underway before dawn, bumping, jolting and crashing along, adding bruises to the bruises.

When daylight showed us the landscape we were driving through, it came as a shock. We might have been on Mars, or the Moon. Outside the windows of the Jeep was a *lunar landscape*. There was not a scrap of vegetation to be seen anywhere around.

The road followed a massive, flat-floored valley, running alongside a winding river bed. There was very little water in the river. The high mountains on either side of the valley were ominous, deeply scarred by ancient water courses, their sides dappled by scree falls.

Was this really Tibet? Where *was* everybody? We hadn't passed a dwelling place in hours. Where were the gangs of Yak I'd been looking forward to seeing? Where were the monasteries?

We drove through that landscape all day, and the only change was that we gained altitude. We began to feel the effects of the height we had reached. In the evening we arrived at a village. Again, it seemed to be just a collection of ramshackle dwellings, surrounded by heaps of stones and rubbish.

We found the hotel, (did I say 'hotel'??) and climbed the broken and dirty steps up to our rooms, stepping over the broken and dirty lino on the way. There was no lock on the Ladies' toilet, so as there was no one around I trotted into the Gents'. There was a lock there, but it came off in my hand. Oh joy.

I went back to our bedroom and sat on the bed, noting without surprise that there was no mattress. The attempt at wallpaper was hanging off in a dozen places, and the window wouldn't close. I was miserable, disillusioned.

"This can't be Tibet," I said to Tod, "We must have taken a wrong turning somewhere."

He just looked at me.

"Tibet should be green and fertile, with loads of Yaks every-where, and hundreds of monasteries. Not this rubbish heap with no trees," I managed to squeeze out a tear. Tod came over and sat next to me – it always works. He put a comforting arm around me.

"Well, this *is* a budget tour, remember," he told me.

"Couldn't we have paid *more*," I wailed quietly, (the walls were paper thin) "and seen the good parts of the country?"

"I don't think it works like that," he said.

I looked up at him. Yes, the sides of his mouth were pulled slightly up – a sure sign of impending laughter.

"Are you laughing at me?" I said.

"Yes," he said, and we both fell about laughing.

It was very cold in the hotel bedroom so we didn't undress for bed that night, and anyway I wasn't certain whether we'd be alone in the beds – the covers looked dubious, and could have been home to any number of crawling or jumping things.

We didn't sleep well, and were woken in the early hours by two drunken women singing in the street outside. The wandering dogs started to bark and howl at them – who could blame them? This was remote Tibet, for God's sake, not Liverpool city centre on a Saturday night.

I was stiff, aching and tired the next morning, and to add to my misery I had a nose bleed. It wasn't unexpected though, as this is one of the very many symptoms of altitude sickness. We had now reached a height of something like 15,000 feet, and were all aware that we were well out of our bodies' comfort zone. Our travelling companions had begun to suffer with headaches, but Tod and I, having been living at altitude in Salle for some time, fared rather better.

We were on the road again before 5am. And then gradually, miraculously, the landscape began to change. Trees appeared here and there, and the valley floors started to show signs of cultivation. Grass began to cover the hitherto uninviting dry, brown earth, and the stones and boulders previously scattered everywhere across the valley floors, almost disappeared.

The Tibet I'd always hoped to see appeared outside the Jeep windows.

We all let out whoops of joy when we saw our first herd of Yak. The driver brought the Jeep screeching to a halt in the middle of the road – we were the only vehicle for miles around – and we piled out to get a closer look.

Amazing, wonderful. I was absolutely thrilled. Yaks are so calm and collected. They all seemed to be meditating while they munched, and barely spared us a glance. They are much smaller than I'd imagined, a bit longer too (some of them may benefit from an extra pair of legs in the middle) with coats like thick weave carpets, reaching down almost to their hooves. Ah, yes, the hairy Yak legs. Lovely chunky faces, big dreamy eyes, and far away expressions, as if they really *do* know something we don't. I wanted to ask them.

We drove on, and my misery and disillusionment were forgotten. As the panorama became more attractive day by day, so the hotels became smarter. The food was really good too, and we were often spoilt for choice. There was usually a selection of meats on the menu, and any number of delicious Tibetan soups. I began to feel guilty about my all-too-quick initial condemnation of the country.

We drove higher and higher, reaching over 17,000ft. Tod handled the altitude well, but Sharon, Adrian and I had some problems. Altitude sickness is sly, it can attack anyone at all, whether you're super fit or not. It's a lottery. It can also be, and often is, a killer if not recognised and addressed.

My nose bled constantly, and I had trouble getting my breath, especially when I tried climbing up hundreds of steps into ancient monasteries!

As we began the approach to Lhasa the newly constructed road, already very good, excelled itself. We were amazed to see signposts telling us how far it was to Shanghi.

We drove through fertile valleys with updated irrigation systems and hundreds of oddly shaped poly tunnels. There were groups of Yak and sheep everywhere.

We rounded a bend in the middle of nowhere and came suddenly face to face with a yak standing in the road, wearing a very fetching multi-coloured coat, and with ribbons streaming from his head. We stopped, or we'd have hit him, and got out. The Yak's owner left a group of men he'd been sitting with at the side of the road, and ran over to us. He wanted me to sit on the Yak while Tod took my photo, and of course we'd have to pay the man for the privilege. There was no way I was getting on that Yak. And although the creature itself looked completely uncon-cerned, I knew it was just putting on a front, and concealing its true feelings.

Another man ran over to us with a beautiful big dog, typical of the kind found in that area of Tibet. The dog had a massively thick coat, especially around the head, and he was wearing a really odd kind of sticky-out collar, again typical of the area. I don't think he was embarrassed about it, in fact he was really laid back, and posed for several photos, sitting on a wall above a hundred foot drop down to the valley floor below.

We paid the men, thanked their animals, and got back in the Jeep. As we drove away Long Life told us that not so long ago a couple of local villagers had discovered that dressing a Yak up, and standing him on the road at that point would attract the tourists. Every Jeep (not that there were ever very many) would stop for photos, and of course the tourists would pay. It was potentially a lucrative option. However, other villagers got wind of this business, and gradually more and more locals brought more and more yaks and dogs to the spot.

Inevitably perhaps it turned nasty, and became a daily brawl, with locals fighting locals, and dogs squaring up to dogs. The Yaks looked on but didn't join in. They are a peace-loving herd.

Eventually a rota was drawn up, and all agreed to abide by it. Peace reigns at the moment.

A couple of hours outside Lhasa we started to see increased traffic on the road. We were excited at the prospect of reaching the capital, and seeing the Potala Palace, that wonderful building that seems to be a part of the very mountain itself. How on earth did they build it? It was had been the official residence of the Dalai Lamas, and contains the tombs of most of them.

It was hot in the Jeep and our driver – the spitting image of Nick Cotton incidentally – had his window open, providing a welcome breeze. He suddenly said something to Long Life, who looked out the rear window and said to us,

"There's a convoy of cars coming. Probably 'political visitors'."

We knew that to be Tibetan-speak for 'Chinese'.

We all looked back, and saw a line of about fifteen chunky 4x4s coming up behind. They all had darkened windows, and were mostly white, gleaming in the sunlight.

Our driver slowed down and pulled as close into the side of the road as possible, to allow the convoy to pass. We all looked forward again and saw the first few Jeeps in the convoy begin to overtake us, and drive away. Then one of the large, gleaming 4x4s pulled alongside, close to our driver's side, and we saw its back window slide down, until it was fully open.

A large Chinese gentleman, wearing a high-buttoned blue suit, appeared at the car window. Suddenly, he thrust a hand out of the window and threw the contents of a bottle of mineral water in the direction of our driver. Unfortunately, most of the water found its intended target, and our driver was soaked. The car carrying the large Chinese 'gentleman' (I now use that word advisedly) sped away.

"What the hell did he do that for?" I yelled, as we all passed tissues to the driver. No one answered, everyone shook their heads.

We were gobsmacked, as they say up in the north of England. I felt ragingly indignant. When it came down to it, I was indignant for the Tibetan people. What kind of treatment was this?

It took us some little time to put this incident behind us, and it niggled at me for a long time.

We spent two wonderful days sightseeing in Lhasa, and felt privileged to have been able to see that beautiful city and its sights. Then we said bye to Sharon and Adrian – they were leaving by train – and Tod and I took a plane out of Tibet back to Kathmandu.

Tod had been looking forward to the flight because we were to pass over Everest. Imagine that, flying over Everest! Now you probably think, as I did, that Everest would be very easy to spot. You know, big famous mountain, pointy top, snow trail blowing off it, the works.

So there we were, flying along in a small plane, actually a *very* small plane, above a solid sea of cloud, and suddenly these mountain peaks start popping up through the cloud below us. Well, do you know what? One mountain peak looks pretty much like another mountain peak, especially when you're looking down on it.

"That's it, over there," someone shouted, and most of the passengers left their seats en masse, and charged down the aisle to the back of the plane, cameras at the ready, pointed to the left.

Ten seconds later and another shout,

"No, that's it, on the right," and they all charged forwards, and over to the right of the plane, cameras clicking as they went.

I'm sure I saw a film once about disastrous weight redistribution in a plane.

But Tod really wanted a photo of the great mountain, so we joined the scrum, tottering first left and then right as the plane hit air pockets over the mountains, ignoring flailing elbows in our chests, and bad breath down our necks. We took photos of every mountain peak we could see, working on the assumption that Everest must be there somewhere. I even handed my camera to a very nice young man, who had his nose glued to the window, and asked him to keep clicking, while I clicked from the other side of the plane with Tod's camera.

We did actually get some magnificent photos of Everest, the world's highest mountain, but we had to ask a seasoned mountain climber to identify the correct photos for us.

Notwithstanding the 'water throwing' incident, I do have to say that we did not experience any other 'incidents' between Tibetan and Chinese occupants of that wonderful country. We visited many monasteries and were pleased to see that they certainly seem to form the hub of Tibetan community life. We had the opportunity to meet and speak with several Tibetans, as well as Long Life and our driver, and we were interested to hear their views about their present way of life. Much of what they said surprised us.

We arrived back in Kathmandu with wonderful memories of our trip to Tibet, and we felt re-energised, ready for and looking forward to our next 'stint' in the village.

Chapter Eleven

On our return from Tibet to Kathmandu we needed to extend our visas, but the thought of a visit to the Immigration Office filled us with dread.

The monsoon, habitually due in June, had failed to materialise yet this year, and the weather in Kathmandu was dry and very hot at that time.

In fact the temperature, in the high thirties, made walking anywhere in the city more of a nightmare than usual. After just a short time outside we were sweating, our t-shirts sticking to us, and our faces, hands and clothes were covered in grime and dust blown up from the roads, and from the piles of rubble and rubbish that lined or obstructed most streets.

The heat was exacerbating other, ongoing problems – the drainage, such as it is, smelled so bad that it took your breath away every few yards, and water was becoming scarce. The newspapers were full of articles about dangerously poor water quality, and there were reports of several cases of Nepalese people becoming ill due to water borne infections. Thank God for our state-of-the-art water-filter bottles!

It was so hot at night that we had trouble sleeping in our hotel room. I wasn't sure if our insurance would cover us for severed body parts, so we didn't leave the ceiling fan on over our bed for too long, in case its maintenance check was due, if indeed it had ever had one.

But our visas had only two days left to run, so we made enquiries, found out approximately how much we'd have to pay, and where we should go at what time.

We took a taxi to the Immigration Office. The hotel receptionist, a nice chap, said we could walk it in forty minutes. However, let me tell you that when talking about distances, altitudes, or getting from here to there, all Nepalese lie. They can't help it. Whopper telling is a national failing.

There are no such words as 'up', 'high', 'climb' and 'difficult' in the Nepali dictionary, so if a Nepalese tells you its an easy trek, you can be sure that's a lie.

Ask them how steep an ascent is and they will give you the standard reply of *"Little bit up, little bit down"*. This neatly replaces *"Very steep, very difficult, probably have to climb"*, none of which will you find in any Nepali dictionary.

So, as the receptionist uttered the words, "Forty-minute walk," his nose grew considerably longer, and we left the hotel and took a taxi.

Good move as it turned out. We'd never have found the Immigration Office ourselves.

Our taxi ploughed out into the morning traffic, and for twenty minutes ducked, dived, squeezed through impossibly small gaps between all manner of vehicles, ignored red lights, shot across junctions, and for the piece de resistance knocked a cyclist off his bike.

No harm done luckily, and three minutes later everyone was back into the usual mayhem.

We turned off the main road and up a steep dirt track, stopping outside a sleazy-looking building. Our taxi driver agreed to wait for us. Round the back of the building we found a sign telling us we were in the right place, and we climbed the stairs to the first floor.

The room was surprisingly small, and there were no more than half a dozen people seated in the waiting area. A wooden counter served as a partition, and behind it, grouped around a simple wooden table, sat seven or eight equally wooden Immigration clerks. On the table was a pile of ledgers, and the clerks were hand writing the visa forms and sticking them in passports. No sign of a phone in the office, and certainly no computers, word processors, or fax machines.

But what did we expect?

As soon as we entered the room three employees rushed out from behind a desk and propelled us to seats by a small table. They produced application forms, and asked us what kind of visas we wanted. On hearing our request, one of them instantly click-clacked on an antiquated-looking calculator and said,

"13,900 Rupees".

"Where does that figure come from?" I asked, "and does it take into account the eight days we have spent out of the country?"

"13,900 Rupees," all three repeated in unison, completely ignoring my question.

Right.

There were notices on the walls stating that we would be given the figure we should pay in American dollars, so I said

"How much is that in dollars?"

Further click-clacking, and a figure was produced.

"Are you sure?" I asked.

Much head-nodding and jabbering.

"What's up?" Tod asked me.

"Well, I don't know what today's exchange rate is, but on yesterday's rate what they're asking is at least 2,000 Rupees too much," I told him. I turned back to the waiting men.

"OK," I said, "We'll pay in dollars."

"No, no, no, no," the three said, all together, lots of head shaking.

"Hummm. I suspect they're telling us we can't pay in dollars," I said.

"13,900 Rupees," the three jabbered at us.

"We haven't got enough Rupees," I told them, "we'll have to change some money."

I'd obviously uttered a few magic words, and I was pretty sure it wasn't any of 'we'll have to change some' because the three stooges turned as one and pointed to the door through which we'd entered.

"The Bank," they said, "five minutes' walk".

Oh yeah, sure it is. All three noses were just about brushing the window on the other wall.

"Come on," Tod said, "We have to change some money anyway, so it may as well be here."

We left the building, checked that our taxi driver would wait for us, and trotted off down the dirt road, and into the noisy mayhem that was the Kathmandu rush hour. Crossing the three-lane road was the least of our problems, because actually managing to walk along the overcrowded opposite pavement turned into the worst kind of dodgem ride. Every way you turned someone or something was waiting to trip you up, scrape your shins, or assail your nose with a smell worse than you could ever imagine.

We battled on for twenty minutes and then saw the Bank. Just our luck – they did not change currency.

We decided to go back to our hotel, have a cold drink, and then get some more accurate information on extracting a visa extension from the Nepalese bureaucracy.

Our taxi driver was more than happy to drive us back to the hotel and then return us to the visa office later on. The conversation with him took place as we drove back down the steep dirt road, with our driver turned round in his seat, and *facing* us in the back. Just in time, over his shoulder, Tod and I saw a tiny puppy ambling across the road in front of the moving taxi.

"Stop!" we yelled together, and thank God the taxi jerked to a stop, with the puppy inches in front of the rusty bonnet.

Neither driver nor puppy were fazed – fazing rarely takes place in Nepal, for any reason.

Tod got out and fished in his pocket for the doggie goodies that we always carry with us. He crouched down, and dropped the bag in front of him on the dusty clay ground. The puppy's head was into the bag before Tod could pull anything out of it, so he just sat back and waited.

A few seconds of noisy and excited rooting and the puppy emerged with a piece of mushroom pizza hanging from his mouth, almost to the ground. He trotted off between two crumbling one-storey houses, and disappeared round the back, past piles of rubbish, to have his breakfast. There's a good chance that it may in fact have been his breakfast, lunch *and* tea.

Once back at our hotel we had a sit down and a cold drink, then we crossed the road to the agency which had organised out trip to Tibet. The manager spoke excellent English, and was bright and obliging. He was pleased to help, and made a few phone calls on our behalf. So, armed with the correct information, we got back in the taxi for a second attempt at visa extraction.

This time we refused to speak to the three stooges, and went instead to the partition, behind which the clerks were still writing. We called over to them, and eventually one of them came over to us. We showed him our completed forms, and he pointed to a woman at the end of the partition, counting money.

"Pay her," he said.

So we joined a queue of three or four other foreigners waiting to pay, and exchanged raised eyebrows and gentle headshakes with them – the universal language of the helpless foreigner, caught in the grip of a baffling bureaucracy.

When our turn came we paid, and received a small ticket with 4pm stamped on it. It was 12 noon, so ok, we'd come back at 4pm to collect our passports, complete with new visas.

Before we made it to the exit the three stooges were back, blocking our way, and surprise surprise, for the sum of only 1000 Rupees they could fix it for us to pick our completed passports up in only twenty minutes.

Now I have to say this proposal held a certain allure. We were hot, tired and hungry, and the thought of going back to the hotel, and coming back to the visa office for a third time, through the noisy, grimy, overcrowded roads was like scraping your nails down a blackboard until your teeth were on edge.

But we knew well that there is a massive problem of corruption in Nepal, reaching greedy, grasping fingers into just about every walk of life, and the unstable on-off government of the moment cannot hope to adequately address the problem.

So we pushed past the three charmers, and were pleased to see the looks of astonishment they gave us as we left the building. One of them followed us downstairs shouting,

"You will have to come back and wait maybe an hour, but if you give me 1000 Rupees only I can fix it in twenty minutes."

We said nothing, got in our taxi, and endured the return journey in the midday heat. We cheered ourselves up with half a dozen spirited, though not too tuneful renderings of 'Mad Dogs and Englishmen' in the back of the taxi. The driver seemed to enjoy it.

After lunch our happy taxi driver – he'd probably made three or four days' wages from us in just one day – took us back again to the visa office. In we went for the third time. We fared not too badly. The payments woman had not given us a receipt for the fee we had paid, so we had to remonstrate with a wall of head-shaking clerks – there's a lot of it about there – before we were actually given our passports back. Then, our new visas had different expiry dates on them.........

But, in the scheme of things this made little difference, and after rescuing Tod from an Immigration clerk who wanted to teach him meditation at the birthplace of Buddha, we left the building clutching our passports, complete with extended visas.

We were not sleeping too well. The night-time temperature seemed hardly any cooler than it had been in the day, and we were bog-eyed and not refreshed in the mornings. Most of Kathmandu seemed to be sleeping on their balconies, and the ragged roar of communal snoring throughout the night was enough to bring tears to your eyes.

Still, a good cold shower went a long way towards waking us

up – not that there was any choice – it was cold or cold, so we settled for cold. The electricity supply to Kathmandu is abysmal, and is *off* much more than *on*, affecting both heating and lighting of course, to say nothing of internet connections. We were eternally grateful to the friends who had given us solar torches and 8-hour candles (how cool is that?) we never went anywhere without them.

Sharon and Adrian told us they had sent a lot of items back to New Zealand by post from Kathmandu, at a surprisingly reasonable cost. This seemed to us a good idea; we'd be able to free up some space in our rucksacks. All we needed to do was to go to the main Post Office and check the details.

We made enquiries, and were told the Post Office opened at 9.30am. So we did the usual bargaining with a taxi driver regarding the fare, and off we went.

Many of the roads in the tourist area of Kathmandu are little more than narrow alley ways, and the mostly ramshackle buildings on either side of the alleys overhang and shadow the uneven and potholed clay surface of the road. The ground floors of most of the buildings in the alleys are shops, with their goods displayed on tables or boards visible through the open shutters, most projecting out into the alley. Any car driving along these alleys passes within a whisker of the displayed merchandise, but we have not yet seen a car exit an alley covered in vegetables or underwear.

Many of the alleys are not even passable in a car, either because there are piles of rubble, or worse, across the route, or because someone, at some time or another, has dug a hole in the middle to reach the drains. Having exposed the drains, and deposited piles of earth and rock liberally in no particular order across the alley, the hole then becomes an old family friend, and is welcome to stay.

We knew where the Post Office was, and we knew that the shortest route to it was via several narrow alleys, so we weren't surprised when the taxi turned down one and shot along it at the speed of light.

We held on in the back, weathering the crashes and bangs like old troopers who knew the score. We skidded round the corner at the end of the alley, and entered another.

Two seconds later the taxi driver jammed his breaks on and we halted abruptly. The reason was immediately obvious. Most of the alley ahead had disappeared into a friendly, drain-searching hole, and the rock and rubble from it was piled up steeply on the hole's left, leaving what looked like just a couple of feet clear between shop front and rubble pile.

The driver banged his hand on the steering wheel and said something. It was probably, "Oh dear, what a nuisance. Someone inconsiderate has dug a hole in the alley."

We waited.

"OK," he said in a loud voice, and put the car in gear. We both craned round to check out the back window and tell him if the way was clear. Off we went with a rush, forwards.

By the time Tod and I had righted ourselves we'd hit the rubble with the front-right tyre, and had begun to tilt sharply to the left.

"Oh my God!" I said, none too quietly, from my position crammed uncomfortably against the left door, *"We're going to turn over!"*

"No, no, no, no," our driver cried, "I drive slowly".

"OK then, we're going to turn over slowly. Will that be better?" I shouted back above the noise of tyres crunching over rock and rubble.

I'd rarely seen the world from this angle, and I didn't much like it. The surface of the alley seemed only inches away from my face, through the car window. Tod started to laugh. He was scrunched up against me, held there by the impossible angle of the car's tilt, and he saw the funny side.

"I'm not giving him a tip," I said, and Tod laughed even more.

We finally reached the end of the pile of rubble and crashed down onto relatively flat ground. I straightened my ruffled feathers and was peeved to see that Tod was still smiling. It'd take a lot more than that to faze him.

Shortly afterwards we arrived at the main Post Office, and followed the appropriate signs round the side of the large rambling building, towards the parcels office.

We were appalled at the piles of rotting rubbish in evidence round the building, and the stench was sickening, made worse by the heat.

Wouldn't you know it – the office we wanted didn't open until 10am, so we got back in our waiting taxi and went back to the hotel.

We made the return journey later in a different taxi, which took a different route, so no car tilting that time. We carried our parcels round the building and into the parcels office.

Wrong office.

We climbed a flight of stairs, trying to ignore the stench of urine that hung over it, and entered a large wooden room – wooden floor, wooden walls, wooden ceiling, large wooden counter, and Post Office clerks to match.

Our side of the counter was packed with a motley assortment of people, and as we waited we realised that none of them were customers. Two or three had just woken up, and were picking ragged blankets up from the floor; some of them were eating and drinking together in the far corner; and the rest were simply sitting on upturned boxes, or the floor, or standing watching what was going on behind the counter.

We were providing an unexpected distraction, and I could feel the weight of many curious pairs of eyes on us.

Eventually a clerk ambled over, took our parcel and weighed it on a creaking, antiquated scales, and then worked something out with a pencil on a scrap of paper. When he told us what it would cost, we were surprised it was so expensive.

"Ordinary Air Parcel or Sea will be cheaper," he told us, "Room 213."

So off we trotted and wandered about the building until we found Room 213. It looked very much like the room we'd just been in, and held much the same kind of audience, who stared at us in much the same kind of way.

Air Parcel turned out not to be any cheaper, and Sea parcel was only marginally so. We decided not to bother, and carried our parcels back to the taxi.

The taxi driver was an obliging kind of chap and, with our permission, took us back to the hotel the 'scenic' way. Very nice, although his chosen route included driving across Durbar Square, the city's most famous square. As we did so I had a more than sneaking feeling that this wasn't really allowed, but hey, this was Kathmandu, not London....

The last of our 'chores' while we were in Kathmandu was to buy our bus ticket back to the village. We knew we'd have to go to the central Bus Station for this, not something we were looking forward to at all, but we felt we couldn't put it off any longer. Time was going on. It was Wednesday the next day, and we wanted to travel on Saturday.

However, Nepal was in something of a political turmoil at that time, and as luck would have it a general strike was called for the Wednesday. That meant no shops, no transport, no taxis, and no government offices.

It was a breathlessly hot day, so we spent most of it sitting in the shade in the hotel's small garden, reading and listening to the occasional running riot outside. When we thought all the demonstrations had passed we went out for a walk, but even in the early evening it was still uncomfortably hot, and eerily quiet along the usually overcrowded and noisy streets. We stepped over a few broken bricks – remnants of the day's politically inspired anger – and made our way back to the hotel.

The next day we asked a taxi driver for a price to the Bus

Station and back.

"You want to go to the *Bus Station*?" he asked, looking at us doubtfully.

"Yes," we said.

"The *Bus Station*?" he said.

"Yes," we repeated.

"Why?" he asked.

Odd question, we thought,

"To buy a ticket," we said.

"Ahh" he said, "So you're going to the ticket office?"

"Yes," we said.

"In the Bus Station?" he asked.

"Yes," we said.

"Do you know where it is, the ticket office in the Bus Station?" he asked.

"No," we said.

"For just a little bit more Rupees I will lead you there," he said, "You may find that useful."

We were certain we *would* find that useful, and accepted his offer.

We hopped into the taxi and off we went.

Kathmandu Bus Station is not in the central city, as you'd imagine, but on a wide, dusty, chaotic road outside.

Buses begin shoving and pushing to get into the Bus Station at quite a distance from the entrance. We couldn't get near, let alone find anywhere to park, so the driver decided to go round the back. Once there, we drove slowly along a clay road, which was really no more than a jumble of potholes and scattered rocks, lined with small open fronted shops on both sides, selling all manner of items from odd-looking, brightly coloured food stuffs to clothes.

Crowds of people spilled out of the shops and across the road, making our somewhat bumpy progress even slower. Every so often, amongst the milling crowds, we came across a cow, calmly meditating in the road, and had to detour around her.

What a life, eh? Lying in the road all morning, blocking the traffic, meditating, and wondering what all the human rush and noise is about. I envy the cows their far away thoughts.

We eventually parked within sight of what I assumed was the back entrance to the Bus Station, and Tod and the driver got out. I would have got out too if the door had opened, but the lock must have been broken, so it remained obstinately shut despite my best efforts. By the time I'd dragged myself across the back seat to the other door, and untangled myself from the elephant and giraffe seat-mats which insisted on coming with me (very popular on back seats of taxis, but for some reason they always become attached to my trousers, and I have been known to exit a taxi wearing one on my bum) Tod and the driver had been swallowed up in the masses of people swirling around the car and along the road.

Amazing how panic gets you moving, and I was out the door in a flash and galloping in unladylike fashion after them. They were only a matter of feet away, unseen in the melee, waiting for me.

We walked into the Bus Station through the massive open steel gates, and were immediately enveloped in the chaos that prevails there.

In Kathmandu Bus Station you will find no ranks of clean, neatly parked buses waiting at their designated bays.

You will see not one single sign telling you which bus is parked where, and why.

You will see not one number, or destination on a bus.

You will however see a tangled mass of mostly rusty, frequently bald tyred, monster size buses jumbled together in no particular order, most of them belching filthy black pollution from infrequently tended engines.

You will witness stand-offs between monster buses vying for space to park.

You will notice buses left unattended and blocking entrance or exit routes, and if you wait a few minutes you may well see someone break into the driver's cab and let the handbrake off, if indeed there is one. Buses without handbrakes on can be moved.

And under all this chaotic, polluted and noisy machine-mayhem lies the human tragedy of the Bus Station People.

Who knows how many people live rough in the Station, sleeping alongside, and in some cases under the buses, night after night. You will see them huddled there.

There is a water tap at one side of the Station, and if it's working you will see them washing there.

Other people come into the Bus Station on a daily basis, to sell a variety of goods and food. Some set up tables amongst the buses, others walk round touting their wares.

And of course you can't fail to notice the people waiting to get on the buses, although God knows it is one of the great mysteries of the Universe, how the hell they know which bus is which, and for where they are bound.

For the most part prospective passengers, often accompanied by chickens and goats, sit on the ground or stand next to a bus, in a patient huddle.

When the bus doors open the huddle is instantly transformed into an aggressive, pushing, shoving, sometimes shouting gaggle until, that is, everyone is seated, and then harmony returns.

The stench that hangs over Kathmandu Bus Station is made up of contributions from most of the above. Early in the morning the uninviting smell of human waste prevails. As the day proceeds this will be overtaken by overpowering, throat-closing fumes from exhausts, mixed with just about any other disagreeable smell you care to imagine.

Conversation is usually impossible in the Station, unless you shout above the incessant roar of the engines.

Tod and I walked behind our taxi driver as we set off to cross the Station. I realised I'd forgotten to bring our face masks – they are becoming standard wear now on the streets of Kathmandu – and they might have given our delicate noses some protection, to say nothing of our lungs.

We picked our way over piles of human excrement, round piles of stinking rubbish, scarily behind monster buses, and quickly in front of them. The taxi driver wasn't hanging around, and we were almost running to keep up, watching where we put our feet all the time. We weaved and zigzagged, and tried not to breathe in.

And then we were across and out onto the other side of the Station, where we finally arrived at the ticket office, neatly hidden in one corner.

Our driver pushed his way through some fifteen or more men who were congregated around the ticket-office window. We followed, and the men stared at us curiously as they moved aside.

An animated discussion began between the ticket-office clerk and our driver, with contributions from most of the men standing around.

We waited. And waited. Nothing moves fast there, and much talking is always involved. So we waited.

Eventually our driver turned to us and said,

"You can't buy the ticket until tomorrow.,"

Right-oh.

So we went back the next day and did it all again.

Chapter Twelve

The journey back to the village again was pretty uneventful, even the music in the mini bus was reasonably muted, and we could speak, as opposed to shouting at each other.

Kalyani and a couple of willing helpers, friends of hers from the village, met us at the Village of the Damned, and although we had very little in our rucksacks they grabbed them and carried them down the mountain for us. It was always useless to protest -- Nepalese women are very strong-minded.

It was a good day for descending a mountain (I've always wanted to be able to say that), not too hot, so we took our time and enjoyed the walk. Kalyani brought us up to date on all the village news and gossip, and we stopped in Lohrimani along the way for a chat with her aunts, uncles and assorted neighbours.

We were welcomed like old friends, and we in turn were truly glad to see them all again. After drinking tea we continued on to the village of Salle, and were again welcomed like long-lost friends on our arrival there.

It was back to work the next day, and we did our usual Pied Piper bit along the path to the school, collecting children in our wake as we went.

The school, Dharmasthali English School, had something like eighty children registered there, although not all of them were able to attend every day. It consists of two small, one-storey wooden buildings divided into five classrooms in all. There is no electricity, and no water in the school.

Survival is the number-one priority up there in the mountains, and to that end each child has to help out with crops, animals, and household chores, and this takes priority of course over their schooling. It would surely give you pause, as it did us, to see tiny children, or old ladies for that matter, carrying sacks of potatoes on their backs up the mountain in the pouring rain, or climbing high trees to chop fresh greens for the goats. This has to be done on a daily basis, as there is no available grazing land.

We ignored the classroom yawns. We understood.

But you know, apart from these necessary absences, the attendance rate is practically 100%. The children don't play truant from school.

Imagine it, a world without television; the internet; computer games; cinemas; DVDs; CDs. A world bereft of bicycles; cars; roller blades; skate boards. A world in which you *can't* just go ice skating, horse riding, dancing, yachting, or shopping. A world in which the question, 'What did you do at the weekend?' (and of course we're talking a *one day* weekend here), usually receives a response along the lines of,

'I did the laundry, and helped my mother cook,' or, 'I worked in the fields and fed the water buffalo.'

School, in that mountainous area, is not just a place to learn something; it is also a place to meet up with your friends. Indeed, for many of the children it is their *only* chance to get together with their friends, as they may well live at a considerable distance from anyone else.

The school seems to have been dropped onto the mountain side in the most beautiful of settings, surrounded by dramatically high mountains and forest. There is a very large flat area around it, ideal for games, and also for foraging for the water buffalo and goats that wandered across it every day. They used to stop to drink from the pond that formed there when the rains came.

All the lessons are conducted in English, except for Nepali language classes of course, and we quickly realised that none of the children, and three out of the four teachers, had never actually heard a native English speaker. This produced some truly bizarre pronunciation!

However, what really threw me was the fact that the children *functioned as a group*. I taught the oldest class, aged from ten to thirteen. The ten children in it were bright, lively, funny, polite, wonderful little people, but they simply did not want to speak English alone, without the participation of the *whole* class. Literally, an individual child simply could not manage to speak alone, and their excruciating embarrassment when asked to do so, was painful to witness.

We tried, and we tried. We set up role plays, we chucked a ball around, we tried games, we enlisted Kalyani's help, but even when she, as a last resort threatened them with a fate worse than death, it made no difference. They would speak together, like a little flock of timid parrots, or not at all. This is in fact how every other lesson in the school is taught, so we should have realised that English would be no different. The children learn everything by rote, and repeat everything together as a class.

OK. Change of plan.

I sat down with Kalyani and devised a different approach to the teaching.

We had already split up the day-long class into child-friendly bites, and we now mixed English grammar, vocabulary, reading and writing, with games and sport. These ranged from indoor games designed to teach, to riotous outside games and sport, designed more for fun.

Bingo! We managed to get the balance right, and I think the appropriate expression is 'we lit the blue touch paper' and watched the 'explosion'.

Tod taught the children games such as rounders, relay racing, wheelbarrow racing, leapfrog, and several of his own inventions, all of which were new to them. He made them a net so they could play volleyball, and he repaired and renovated two old quoits.

The noisy fun and laughter from our class outside always attracted the attention of those children left inside the little school, in other classes, but Kalyani was happily in favour of all the children who were old enough joining in.

I have rarely seen anything funnier than a mass leapfrog race, girls versus boys. There were some spectacular pile ups! But never any tears.

One of the kids' favourite games was 'Simon Says', and I'm sure Tod sometimes regretted teaching it to them, as he was mobbed almost daily to play it with them. They got so good at it that we often had to concede defeat, or we'd still have been there late into the night.

Imagine the scene -- a hot afternoon high in the remote Himalayas, blue sky, blazing sun, a small isolated school surrounded by forested mountains, twenty small children outside, standing holding hands in a circle. Then, amid much loud squealing and laughter what do they do? *Yes*, the Hokey Cokey.

I'm afraid we *did* teach it to them.

The children's enthusiasm for competitive sport knew no bounds, and they approached every game in a spirit of deadly seriousness. The girls usually won at everything, much to the boys' annoyance. We asked the boys one day to choose a game with a view to getting their own back on the girls. What do you know, they chose football.

So, in that idyllic setting, Tod marked out the football field and the goals, and off they went.

The boys never stood a chance. The girls are better at organising themselves, much better disciplined, and in the case of the footy match they appeared to pack a much harder punch than the boys. Tod had to wade in and rescue one little boy who had disappeared under a screaming mob of girls, every one of them hell bent on getting the football from him at any cost.

We watched open-mouthed and cringing as the girls chopped the legs out from under any boy who stood in their way, using elbows and feet indiscriminately.

This was the pattern in any of the competitions which we set up – win at any cost. And that included cheating, which was rife on both sides of any game, test or competition, if they thought they could get away with it.

Tod made them a game of bamboo rings which are thrown from a distance, hopefully to land over a stick fixed in the ground. Hoopla, I think it's called. The children had never seen anything like that, and threw themselves on it with their usual competitive enthusiasm. Unfortunately for the boys (again) two of the girls in particular were excellent at that game, and we had to break up several shouting arguments as a result.

We tried 'hide and seek' with them, and after a count of one hundred, said in English at the speed of light, the eight 'seekers' propelled themselves out of the classroom door like a pack of whippets out the traps, screaming and baying, trampling Kalyani into the dust as they went. We eventually had to remove 'hide and seek' from the agenda when, one day, after thirty minutes of 'seeking' the one remaining 'hider' was found high up at the top of a fir tree, which was growing perilously close to the side of the mountain.

Mind you, 'Health and Safety' would have had a field day with us anyway. We hid some objects in the classroom one day, and watched in awe as girls and boys alike swung across the overhead beams, climbed the walls, and clung by fingertips to the top of the blackboard in a frenzied search for the hidden objects, screaming and laughing all the way.

During races some of the children had spectacular falls, and would hit the hard clay ground at speed, disappearing for a moment under a cloud of dust. But they'd just get up, brush themselves down and join in the game again.

We tried to introduce them to drawing, and Tod set up several still life scenes. Kalyani loved the idea, so we had a 'whole school' competition, which produced some amazingly good sketches. There were some hilarious moments though, and for me none more so than the day I asked the class to sketch Tod's feet, in his walking boots.

For twenty minutes Tod sat unmoving at the front of the class while the kids scribbled and concentrated in silence. Then they showed us the results of their labours. They had produced ten almost identical sketches of Popeye-type legs and feet! *Where did that come from??*

Cheating, as I've mentioned, was an accepted way of school life there in the mountains, and to be honest it was so blatant that it was funny. There were only two, very out-of-date English/Nepali dictionaries in the school, and the children didn't know how to use them. Having taught them how to look up words, something which they found very easy to do, the dictionaries then slid into use as cheating aids in spelling tests.

We took umpteen photos of the children and the school, and this probably took us twice as long as it would have done in the UK. The kids were fascinated by our cameras, and crowded round us whenever they spotted one. Each time we took a photo we had to show them the picture on the camera, and they would stare, point and laugh, absolutely delighted with it every time. Eventually, as soon as they spotted us with a camera the children would leap into a smiling group and stand stock still, posing, waiting for the click.

We began to find it hard to get natural photos of them. We spent one morning photographing the whole school, class by class with their teachers, and then a complete school shot. Yes, it took us a morning to do it.

We showed our class a pair of binoculars one day. They had no idea what they were, so we all went outside, and the kids took it in turns to look around through the binoculars. They were absolutely fascinated. Kalyani had also never seen binoculars, so she brought the whole school out, class by class, to look through them. It became known as 'The Great Binocular Morning'.

There were so many wonderful, touching and funny moments with the children, but amongst them all I think the day Tod made a *see-saw* for them is my favourite.

Unfortunately, someone in the valley had realised that timber was in demand in Kathmandu, and with the recent extension of the track to an accessible point above the village timber from the valley could be loaded onto trucks and sold to dealers. So the felling of trees in the forest around Salle began. While we were there it intensified, and on two occasions our path to the school was blocked by toppled trees.

Kalyani told us that the forest was 'common land', and that in fact this tree felling was not legal. The new Nepalese government had begun to look into the potential environmental damage it could cause, as tree felling for financial gain was becoming big business in many parts of the country, and there was no system of reforestation in place.

We began to notice stray logs, left by groups of tree fellers, on the paths and mountainside along the route to school. One day Tod spotted a pile of abandoned logs high above the path, and suddenly had the idea of using one of them to make the children a see-saw.

We decided that Tod and I, with Kalyani helping, would climb up the mountainside to where the logs had been dumped, and bring a suitable see-saw-sized one back down to the playground. The three of us together should be able to carry it. We told Kalyani our idea, and it was decided we'd go during the morning break.

Break time came, the children rushed outside, and as Kalyani was nowhere to be seen Tod and I sat inside and waited. Ten minutes later she stuck her head round our classroom door and said

"OK. All is organised." She was grinning.

We looked at her blankly.

"The children," she said, "Your class, I've sent them to get the log."

"What?" I said, "But how will...."

"Don't worry. I've told them Tod and Fiona want a log, so they've gone to get you one."

"How will they manage to carry it?" I asked. I felt a bit

panicky; we were talking up a mountainside here, and more to the point, *down* a mountainside.

"They'll manage," Kalyani said, still grinning.

I followed Tod outside. He was already standing in the middle of the playground looking up into the forest, towards the point where we had seen the abandoned lengths of wood.

"Listen," he said, and in the distance, from up in the forest, I could hear the unmistakable sound of children's laughter, with the odd squeal here and there.

"Let's go and help them," I said. I had visions of the log cannoning off the edge of the mountain, accompanied by half a dozen of our class. What would we tell the parents?

"Let's just see if they can do it," Tod said.

"But by the time we're in a position to say '"No they can't do it, let's go and help'" we may be down a child or two in class," I said.

Kalyani put her arm through mine and said,

"What is it that you often speak about? Problem solving? Confidence building?" she was still grinning.

"Actually, this wasn't quite what I had in mind," I told her.

There was a sudden crashing and cracking noise from the forest, and amidst much shouting and laughter the chosen log made a spectacular entrance, rolling at speed down the mountainside towards the path. The kids were running to keep up with it.

"Humm," Tod said, "I wonder how they're going to stop it."

He had a point. If the log made it to the path and kept on going, it would simply drop over the edge and disappear down the mountain. Flattened goats and crushed crops sprang alarmingly to mind.

"Oh, I wouldn't worry," I said, "a couple of the kids will probably throw themselves in front of it. That should stop it."

Tod gave me a withering glance. He has mentioned on more than one occasion that sarcasm doesn't become me.

But guess what, just before the log reached the path it was confronted by a tight little group of children, and they managed to block its onward progress. Incredibly, the only damage done was a scraped shin.

The children were having a great time, and they got the log moving again towards the playground. They suddenly spotted my camera, and before you could say 'photo opportunity' they were all in position, smiling and posing on the log.

Tod directed proceedings as the log reached its destination, and the kids scurried off to find a number of items – four pieces of wood to be used as stakes to keep the log in place; something flat and hard to hit the stakes with and drive them into the ground; and a plank which had not been needed when the seating benches had been installed in the school. They were back in no time at all with everything required. We were really proud of them.

Kalyani helped Tod set the see-saw up, while I stood with the kids and watched proceedings. The children were still not too sure exactly what Tod was building, but when it was ready Kalyani and I got on it and attempted to show them how it was done. They were thrilled. They loved it, and in no time at all we had multiple kids on each end of the see-saw, and the sound of their squealing and laughter echoed round the mountains. Kalyani brought the rest of the school out and everyone had a go on it, teachers too.

That day became known as 'The Great See-Saw Day'.

Chapter Thirteen

Tod, known to everyone as Ali Baba because of his beard, also became widely known as Doctor Tod.

It was a good thing that we had taken a large supply of basic medication with us to Nepal because in the village, where absolutely no medication is available, we were asked to help with a huge number of different ailments and accidents.

There was not even an aspirin in the village, and the nearest medical help was at the hospital in Jiri – twelve kilometres along the road from The Village of the Damned – that is, of course, after climbing the mountain to get up to the road.

Most villagers did not have the necessary bus fare anyway, so in the case of a baby which had fallen on its head, and a woman who had a badly infected dog bite, Tod explained that he could do nothing to help, and that it was imperative for them to seek medical attention immediately. We gave them enough money to get to the hospital, but the effort it must have taken for those two women to climb the mountain, and travel to the hospital doesn't bear thinking about.

Almost every day someone would come to our door asking for help. We saw a great many skin conditions, eye infections, ear infections, a nasty spider bite, countless stomach complaints, and a vast number of cuts.

The problem with cuts we found, was that the villagers have a custom of covering a cut with soil. So most of the cuts we saw were already infected, and needed cleaning. We had brought antiseptic cream, cleansers, plasters, painkillers, Imodium, and eye drops with us, but our supplies were all too quickly exhausted. We stocked up again in Kathmandu each time we were there, but we were acutely conscious that what was needed was a regular visit to the village by a medical practitioner. However, there wasn't one for miles around.

The village water supply is poor, as it is in almost all the remote villages of Nepal, and while we were in Kathmandu, as I have already mentioned, we read in the Nepalese newspapers about an increasing national problem of water transmitted illnesses. There is dysentery in the village, and stomach aches and diarrhoea are frequent, in both children and adults.

When the monsoon came, the resulting change in the weather, and the all-pervading dampness meant that many of the villagers, young and old, began to suffer high temperatures and aches and pains.

From time to time Kalyani had pointed out plants growing wild, which were used in traditional Nepalese medicine. I was surprised to find that none of these cures were in use in the village. Maybe they had been forgotten over the years, like the art of cheese-making.

A lot of the villagers kept goats, not for milk, but for breeding and selling on, or exchanging. One morning when we were on the way to school a woman asked Tod to take a look at one of her goats that had a sore hoof. She wouldn't take no for an answer, so Tod had a look. Not knowing if it would help at all he sprayed the hoof with antiseptic spray, and got a nasty look from the poor animal in return. As we passed the house every day on the way to school, Tod sprayed the goat's hoof each morning for a week. It really helped, and the hoof began to heal. But this of course opened the animal floodgates, and we were then inundated with requests to look at other poorly animals, all of which Tod politely declined.

The monsoon rains, when they came, brought the leeches out. What charming little chaps. Their aim in life is to grab anything with a bit of blood in it, and pinch it for themselves.

The paths around the village are one person width, and many quickly became overgrown with rain-encouraged foliage and grass. However, Kalyani told us to stay on the paths, even when that meant wading through thick mud and puddles, in order to give the leeches less chance of latching on to us.

Much as I came to love water buffalos during our stay in the village, I discovered at that time that they lack common courtesy.

This could be as a result of their upbringing, but nevertheless whenever I came nose to nose with one on a narrow path they would never stand aside. However, navigating carefully around a portly water buffalo is actually something I'd recommend. You should try it sometime. They are beautiful creatures.

Leeches, however, are sly and deceitful. They hang on to any bit of foliage, high or low, and wait for any passing blood container. As soon as they land on something unfortunately suitable they latch on, and begin to suck out the blood. When they are full they drop off.

The little buggers were everywhere. We had to stop every five minutes to check that we were leech free. They fall down inside your collar, they climb up your leg from your boots, they land in your hair – and the worst thing is that you don't feel them on you, even when they are dining on your blood, because the crafty little swine secrete an anaesthetic when they latch on to something yummy. As if that's not bad enough, they then release an anti-clotting enzyme into the host, so the blood flows freely. How disgusting is that?

One day I was sitting reading, an hour after coming in, when I suddenly noticed a sizeable lump inside my trouser leg, just below the knee. I now hold the Olympic record for whipping off trousers, and a leech, bloated with my blood, thumped squelchily onto the floor. It looked like a miniature, red inner tube. The perfectly round hole it had made in my leg bled profusely for forty-eight hours.

Woolly Head's glamorous girlfriend was often to be found hanging round our house. One morning as I was stroking her I noticed what I thought was some clay or soil, blocking one of her nostrils. I am short sighted, and no, I didn't have my glasses on, so the world around me was rather blurred. I wiped at the blockage with a tissue but couldn't move it, so I called Tod.

He, being less bat-like than me, saw it was a leech, right up inside the nostril. We chased Miss Glamour round for ten minutes, trying to remove it, but then she decided she didn't like the game and trotted off, leaving a trail of blood spots along the ground as she went.

When we saw her later she was, happily, leech-free and fine. Presumably the leech had drunk its fill and fallen out.

An odd thing. The village paths mostly follow the very edge of the terraces or mountainside, so you are walking right next to a drop of anywhere between ten and one hundred feet, sometimes more. The leeches know this (how cool is that?) and they all begin life on the 'safe' side of the path. Even when the path, unusually, crosses a field or winds through the forest, where there is a choice of sides the little buggers are always to be found on the highest side.

We asked Kalyani why this was, and she said,

"They can see you better of course."

Right-oh.

Up there in the mountains one of the first things you notice is the flies. At first glance you'd think they were your common or garden English-type house flies. Believe me, they are *not*.

In the Himalayas the flies go round in gangs, and there are hundreds of them, everywhere you look. Their mission in life is to pester everyone, human and animal alike.

They do not land sedately on you, they literally fly into you. These Himalayan Hoodies are either incredibly short-sighted, or they have not worked out how to use their brakes. They crash-land in your hair, and then struggle – not a pleasant feeling. Eating is a constant battle, drop your vigilance for a moment and you are munching one of them. Drinking anything is a nightmare – an uncovered cup is an open invitation for a splash about. Everything has to be covered all the time. They fly non-stop directly into your mouth, ears and eyes, and will dash up your nose given the chance.

I have always felt it a mistake to have dispensed with the human tail. Given the prevalence of the Himalayan Hoodies up there in the mountains, I'm surprised not to have spotted a tail or two lurking in a remote village, retained by a benevolent and thoughtful evolutionary process specifically in order to combat those damned Hoodies.

Chapter Fourteen

On our return to the village we were greeted enthusiastically, as usual, by Woolly Head. We could hear his loud, deep bark before we saw him. However, he was holding one leg off the ground as he hobbled determinedly over to see us, and an inspection showed a deep cut and severely swollen knee joint.

Everyone looked shifty in the extreme when I asked how it had happened, but I kept on asking, and was eventually told that 'a man' had hit Woolly.

"Why?" I asked

"We don't know," the villagers told me, looking if anything even shiftier.

My question was in fact a stupid one, as we already knew that no one in Nepal needed a reason to hit or stone a dog. I never found out who the man was, probably because the villagers knew what I'd have done with that information.

We prescribed bed rest for our furry friend, and the woman living next door but one (there were three houses together on the terrace) found Woolly a sheltered place outside her house, and put him on a chain during the day. This solved the constant problem of him following us to school, and helped the healing process on his leg.

She also began providing Woolly with two meals a day. This was just left over rice, but it was something he had never had before on a regular basis. We thanked her every time we saw her put the food in front of Woolly.

The chain, which was placed over a metal stake in the ground, was long enough to allow him to get up onto a wooden cupboard nearby, and sit on top of the woodpile there, surveying the land around.

Woolly became a nosey neighbour – every village needs one.

A couple of days after we got back we decided to walk to Lohrimani, the next village, to buy some Coke. *Yes, Coke!* One or other of the few small 'shops' there sometimes had a couple of bottles.

As we started out, we walked past Woolly asleep on the woodpile. He heard us and made a fuss. He wanted to come with us. But a couple of months previously we had made the massive mistake of letting him accompany us, not realising that there are three bad-tempered, moth-eaten dogs in the village of Lohrimani, and they don't like canine visitors to the village. They set upon poor old Woolly, and we only just managed to extract him in time, before any real damage was done. So, never again.

We turned onto the path at the side of the house and, leaving Woolly barking his head off up on his cupboard, trotted up onto the terraces, and were soon climbing steeply away from the houses. The corn crop was as tall as us by that time, and in places we had to push our way through as it leant across the narrow path. We were on the look out for leeches, and constantly checked each other for them as we walked along.

Ten minutes later and Woolly's barking was still echoing across the valley, we heard a series of loud crashes, and the barking stopped abruptly. Wondering what had happened, we ran a bit further on along the path to an opening between the trees and crops, from where we could look back across the terraces and see the houses.

The woodpile was no longer on top of the cupboard, and nor was Woolly.

"Oh my God, if he's fallen off with the wood he'll have hung himself on the chain," I shouted in a panic, but Tod was already running back along the path, and I started to run after him. We went as fast as we could, which wasn't easy on a narrow, damp and slippy path, with quite a drop on one side. My track record wasn't good along there either.

Then, round a corner up ahead of us came Woolly, hurrying as fast as he could after us on his three good legs. We were as pleased to see him as he was to see us. We checked him over and he appeared to be none the worse for his fall. His chain was still round his neck. How it had lifted off the stake I suppose we will never know. But thank goodness that it did.

We walked him slowly back, and he settled down again, this time on the ground at the side of the house. We pretended to go back into our house, but we actually sneaked quietly round the back, like a couple of burglars, just outside Woolly's line of vision. We reached the path without him spotting us and set off again for Lohrimani.

After that incident, whenever Woolly was on his cupboard we had to sneak round the back of the house. He had ears like a couple of radars. His leg healed well, and the swelling went down quickly. He was back to four paws again pretty soon.

Of course Woolly was never on the chain at night, because he had a job to do, as did every one of his canine colleagues.

A couple of weeks after the 'woodpile incident' I awoke in the darkness of night to the sound of Woolly and his girlfriend barking and snarling. I could tell by the intensity that they really meant business. It was 11.50pm. I lay there and listened. There is something incredibly eerie about the sound of angry barking echoing round the dark and otherwise silent valley. Other dogs, further down amongst the terraces, joined the barking. Something was definitely afoot. And then I heard the elderly couple who live downstairs talking with their neighbour (Woolly's new 'mum') outside the house.

Suddenly they began banging stones on metal plates. What on earth were they doing? I wondered. Someone down the valley started whistling, a loud and piercing sound, adding to the already considerable cacophony. I got up and looked out the glassless window. In the bright moonlight I could see Woolly and his girlfriend standing side by side right at the edge of the flat clay area in front of the house, barking furiously down into the terraces below. Behind them the elderly couple and their neighbour were walking around, banging stones on metal plates, and shouting. Other voices were shouting up from the valley, the noise punctuated by the continuing loud whistling. I wondered *what* they were shouting. I was fascinated. They were laughing together in between the shouting, so I didn't think anything serious was going on. Maybe it was some kind of weird ceremony – a thanksgiving for the arrival of the monsoon? Asking the gods to provide a good harvest? Huumm.

Gradually the dogs stopped barking, and then the couple said goodnight to their neighbour and went back into the house. Apart from Woolly grumbling to himself, silence returned once again to the valley.

I went back to bed. Tod was still snoring.

Just after 2am we had a repeat performance. I got up again, looked out the window, and saw exactly the same scene as before. The valley was filled yet again with shouting, whistling, and the sounds of stone on metal.

Woolly, his girlfriend and several colleagues were barking and snarling, and Woolly was racing up and down the edge of the terrace, his paws pounding on the hard clay.

I could still hear laughter in amongst the jumble of sounds, and again I wondered what on earth they were all doing. What strange moonlight ceremony were they performing?

Abruptly the row stopped, and everyone went back into their houses again. The valley settled down, and silence returned. Strange people, I thought. I too went back to bed. Tod was still snoring.

In the morning when Kalyani arrived with our breakfast, I asked her what kind of ceremony it had been. She looked at me blankly.

"You know," I said, "midnight and 2am, banging on plates, shouting, whistling, dogs barking. What were they doing?"

The blank stare remained.

"The neighbours," I said, "Outside at midnight, lots of noise. Was it a kind of ceremony?"

Kalyani, who lived over the hill at the back of our house, had heard nothing, and didn't know what I was talking about. So she trotted off to ask the neighbours what they had been doing in the night.

A few minutes later she was back, giggling as she climbed into our room through the window.

"There was a tiger outside the house," she announced, "It was probably trying to get the goats. Woolly and the neighbours scared it off.," She was laughing now.

Actually, I didn't really think it was all that funny. I felt a bit of a shiver coming on. I made a mental note to have a quiet word with my bladder. There would definitely be no more nocturnal trips to the outside loo!

'Woolly, my dear brave boy. Step forward while I shake your honourable paw, and pin this medal for "'Gallant Protection of Cowardly Foreigners"' to your fur. God bless you, my boy.'

Chapter Fifteen

A couple of days after we arrived back in the village the monsoon, already several weeks late that year, began in earnest.

We discovered that the monsoon there in the valley involved rain, wet and dangerously slippy paths, rain, vegetation doubling in size overnight, rain, soggy and undryable clothing, rain, hot and sweaty days even in the pouring rain, rain, and in *my* case several spectacular sliding falls, one of which took me to the very edge of a deep ravine.

"God, Fo, what are you doing?" Tod called, an unfamiliar note of annoyance in his voice.

"Nothing much, dear, just looking over the edge here,"

"Well stay on the path will you, and stop playing silly buggers. That's an eighty-foot drop."

"Right-oh, dear. I'll just extricate myself from these handy bamboo stems that have broken my fall, and I'll be right behind you."

I'd got the worst of the mud off by the time we reached the school. Mind you, the children were used to seeing me with patches of mud on various parts of my anatomy, and would sometimes take it in turns to brush me down.

Monsoon season is the leeches' favourite time of year, and they were *everywhere*. They plagued human and animal alike. Children often came into school with blood running down their legs from leech bites, and we frequently saw adults who'd been working (shoeless of course) in the fields, with blood on their feet. But *we* were definitely the only ones around there with a fear of leeches. The villagers looked on with amusement as we hopped around, batting the little buggers off our clothes, and scrutinising the undergrowth.

There were three funerals in the village during our stay. We were invited to all three but politely declined. We didn't know the first two people at all, and had only met the third one, the oldest lady in the village, once, when she came to give us flowers before we set off on a trip away. So, had we attended any of the funerals we would have felt like nosey outsiders, although we knew we would have been treated like honoured guests.

The village of Salle is basically a Buddhist village, although I have to say we saw little or no evidence of religious practice there. The business of living, surviving, takes precedence, and religion has been relegated to weddings and funerals, with religious practice being adapted to fit the way of life.

Following a death, the body of the deceased is carried up the mountain behind the village to the cemetery at the top, usually the day after the death.

Buddhist priests conduct the ceremonies, and the body is cremated, and left for three days, at which time the deceased's close family return to cover over the remains. Sometimes, if the family can afford it, a small stone and clay monument is erected on top.

Horns and drums will sound most of the day and night, accompanying the deceased on its journey to the next life, strange mournful sounds floating out across the valley.

Depending on the position the deceased held in the village, the funeral celebrations may last from one to three days. The last death in the village while we were there was the oldest lady, and she was accorded a three-day celebration.

As I have already mentioned, many of the villagers make their own alcohol, raxi, and it is liberally consumed by men and women alike. Unfortunately, there is a growing problem of alcohol consumption, not just in the village of Salle, but throughout Nepal, and as you may imagine funeral celebrations involve the drinking of copious amounts of raxi throughout the day and night.

Having declined to attend the funerals we did nevertheless want to see the cemetery if at all possible, and we asked Kalyani if we could climb the mountain, and maybe take some photos up there. She and the villagers we mentioned it to, were really pleased that we were interested, and there were no objections to our visiting their cemetery.

Eventually we asked Kalyani for a day off school so we could climb the mountain. Our reasoning for the day off was so that we could take our time, and not attract attention to our quest; just in case any of the villagers should be offended by a couple of strangers visiting their sacred cremation ground.

Not attract attention? Who did we think we were kidding?

The villagers were so pleased that we really did intend going up to the cemetery that the school was closed for the day, allowing any children who wanted to, to come with us. Kalyani and a group of villagers wanted to come too, and everyone dressed up in traditional Nepalese dress to celebrate the occasion.

We were thrilled. So a group of about twenty of us set out early one bright morning.

We collected more and more villagers, adults and children, as we went. The youngest child in our group was eight, and two or three of the ladies were probably in their seventies or maybe even older. As we turned onto the steep path and started to climb, they, as usual, put me to shame. I slithered about on the damp ground in my state of the art walking boots, while they, in sandals, flip flops, or barefoot, climbed sure footedly.

It was a beautiful sunny day, not too hot, just right for walking. The forested mountainside looked a bit like a jungle, and we soon found ourselves pushing through exotic-looking ferns and foliage growing across the path. It was very quiet in the forest.

The children were running about like mountain goats, squealing and laughing, picking wild strawberries and lilies and giving them to Tod and I. Everyone was talking, laughing, and calling to each other as we climbed the steep single-file path.

I just knew that this was a happy memory in the making, one that would stay with me for ever. The villagers' obvious happiness at taking us up to see their sacred place at the top of the mountain really touched Tod and I. Not for the first time we felt humbled.

Every so often I heard Kalyani calling to me from the path below, checking that I was ok. But the villagers were so used to seeing me toppling over this way or that, that I only had to begin to wobble and someone grabbed me!

Oddly enough, since returning from Tibet where we'd reached the mind-boggling altitude of 17,500 feet, I had found breathing, walking and climbing much easier around the village. You know, it was as if my body was saying, 'OK, if you promise never again to take me up to the ridiculous height of 17,500 feet, I'll make life much easier for you here at 7,000 feet.' So we had reached an agreement my body and I, although to be honest, I felt I was being blackmailed.

But for the first time in three months I wasn't puffing, sweating, and trying to persuade my shaky legs to take another stride. In fact I felt great, much to everyone's surprise and amusement, and I didn't need the oft-proffered helping hands to get me up the steeper parts of the path. Yippee.

The route up to the cemetery was very overgrown, and the higher we went the more bushes and trees blocked the way, and had to be pulled aside. Every so often we'd be showered with drops of water from branches as they snapped back into place.

Kalyani's grandfather, an elderly, wise, lovely man had handed out cubes of salt crystal before we set off, and now we saw why. The whole mountainside was alive with leeches, and those sly creatures couldn't believe their luck. They had doubtless never seen that amount of food together in one place, and anticipating a feeding frenzy they began leaping out of the undergrowth, launching themselves from trees, and grabbing at anything that moved past them.

The villagers walked on through, paying little or no attention to the clutching leechy things, except to casually pick them off clothing or skin and chuck them away. They would occasionally apply their salt cubes to those more persistent leeches, with miraculous, instantaneous effect. Leeches hate salt – remember that the next time you are climbing through a forest in Nepal.

Tod and I, on the other hand, became a couple of whirling dervishes, jabbing with our cubes of salt at anything long, thin, or moving on our clothing.

I'd noticed that my glasses had become loose recently, and had taken to slipping down my nose and off my face. I am lost, literally, without my glasses, being one of life's human bats, and I really needed them to behave and stay in place. But wouldn't you know it, they refused, leaving me short-sightedly dabbing with my salt cube, usually missing the intended target.

Tod really does not like leeches at all, and after I'd inadvertently salted his boot lace, instead of the leech that had burrowed into his sock, he asked me to move away. At least, that's what he meant, I think. One of the villagers pulled the leech out, but not before it had drawn quite a bit of blood. Tod does a rather good accusing look.

Kalyani's grandfather led us on up the mountain to the very top, and there we found the cemetery. Perhaps there never was a more serene setting for a sacred place. The cremation smoke does not have far to travel – you are already in the sky. Wisps of mist moved round the cremation mounds and monuments that morning, and the feeling of calm was almost overwhelming.

We wandered around and took photos, and then Kalyani's grandfather led us along the ridge at the very top of the mountain, to an even older cemetery. There he showed us a monument which commemorated his great grandparents. It stands on the highest point of the mountain, and the view all around is spectacularly far reaching.

Then, with Kalyani translating for us, and the children and

villagers standing round quietly listening, her grandfather told us a strange story. This is what he said:

Roughly one hundred years ago, four black men came to the village of Salle. They climbed the mountain, as we had done, and reached the very spot where we were standing. They sat on the monument, and made drawings of the whole area they could see, in every direction.

They did not speak Nepali, and made no effort to communicate with the villagers. No one in the village recognised the language they spoke.

The men were dressed in a similar style to traditional Indian dress, but they were not Indian. They carried swords.

The men stayed two days at the top of the mountain, then they descended by the same path, and left the village. Some time later the villagers heard that they had climbed to the top of each peak in the region.

The identity of those men, and the reason for their visit, remains a mystery to this day.

We came down the mountain along a different path, and stopped at a Temple which had been created around a massive hollow tree. The children rang all the prayer bells hanging there, and we marvelled at their deep sounds as they vibrated round the otherwise silent forest.

Kalyani told us that back in the mists of time a young boy had misbehaved at home, and afraid of the trouble he would be in, and the ensuing punishment, he ran off into the forest to hide. He squeezed into the hollow tree, and some time later was discovered there, dead.

We walked on, and across one of the very few open fields we had seen in the whole area. It was a beautiful, gently sloping area of grass, and Kalyani's grandfather told us that, many years before, when he was a young man, he and some other villagers had grown potatoes there. They used to watch rabbits running through the field while they were working.

In all our time in the village, and in fact in Nepal, we never saw a rabbit.

We did, however, see many spectacularly beautiful birds, and one day we asked Kalyani the name of a lovely yellow bird we had seen.

"Yellow bird," she said.

Some time later we asked her the name of a turquoise bird we'd spotted.

"Turquoise bird," she told us.

A pattern seemed to be developing, so we nipped it in the bud and bought a book on Nepalese birds the next time we were in Kathmandu.

Our day out at the cemetery was wonderful, and we felt privileged to have seen it. We arrived back in the village laden with flowers, and with the children still racing around laughing and playing. They talked about the fun they'd had that day for weeks after. For Tod and me it will always remain a treasured memory.

Chapter Sixteen

The day before we were due to leave the village for good, and return to the UK, the school children and their parents gathered outside the Junior school to wish us well.

It was a hugely emotional day for us, and for many of those present who had become our friends. There were tears but also much laughter.

Kalyani, as headmistress, made a speech thanking us for coming to the school, and for everything we had done during our stay in the village. She had to stop half way through as the tears came.

Then every child, and all the parents, came up to us one by one to put garlands of flowers round our necks, and to place a spot of red tikka on our foreheads. The tradition of placing tikka on the forehead, (it should be applied with the thumb, in one upward stroke), indicates a blessing.

However, by the time eighty small children, many with wobbly aim, had placed tikka on us, Tod looked like a garden gnome, and I looked as if someone had taken a hatchet to me.

We all laughed and laughed. The teachers and founders of the

school presented us with a picture of the Hindu gods. We were touched, and so sad to be leaving.

That evening the local children gathered, as usual, outside the house. But they were joined by several adults this time, all come to say goodbye. The children sang and danced for us, and we sat on the veranda talking with them until late.

We had a constant stream of visitors, as we'd had all that week, most of them bringing raxi, all of them coming to say thank you, and to wish us goodbye. Everyone wanted to know when we were coming back.

When we emerged onto the veranda early the next morning, we were amazed to see a group of villagers already standing silently outside the house. The children were there too, and they came upstairs and stood watching us finalising our packing.

When we were ready, we picked up our rucksacks and, amid cries of 'bye bye, bye bye', we walked up the hill for the last time, round to Kalyani's house. There, another group of villagers, and Kalyani's family, were waiting to say goodbye. It was another emotional farewell, and we were presented with more garlands of flowers, but no tikka!

When the time came to leave it seemed like half the village wanted to walk as far as Lohrimani with us. So, waving a final farewell, and with cries of 'bye bye' echoing all around, we set off in a group of about twenty. It was a beautiful clear day, just right for a long journey.

A couple of minutes later I spotted Woolly trotting along behind us.

"No," I said "*You* can't come," and I tried to grab him, with a view to sending him back to the village. Woolly thought it was a game, and neatly avoided all attempts to corner him.

The men carrying our rucksacks looked on in amusement. Knowing how fond we were of Woolly, they wanted to know why I didn't want him to come with us.

"Because those three moth-eaten thugs in Lohrimani will go

for him again," I said, and waited for Kalyani to translate. Humm, I wonder how you say 'moth-eaten' in Nepali? Or 'thug'?

"They say don't worry," Kalyani said, "They will look after Woolly dog and keep him safe."

"How can they possibly do that?" I said.

But the men had already walked on along the path, and Woolly had run ahead with them. I couldn't catch him. There was nothing I could do.

I did not enjoy that last walk to Lohrimani. It was bad enough that we were leaving the village for good, but I just knew that Woolly would be in big trouble the moment he put his nose into those thugs' territory.

We gathered more people along the way, and by the time we reached the outskirts of the village of Lohrimani our group numbered around thirty. Kalyani's relatives came out onto the street to greet us, and we sat down outside for a breather.

It was only a matter of a couple of minutes before Woolly was spotted, and the locals charged over to have a go at him. Kalyani and I got between Woolly and the moth bags, and they eventually slunk off to a safe distance and sat glaring at Woolly. The men carrying our rucksacks had already got underway again, and were some distance away, heads down, walking quickly towards the mountain path. No help there then.

"I'll take Woolly back to the village," I said to Kalyani, "He doesn't stand a chance here."

One of her aunties came over to us with a thick piece of rope. Woolly, who was leaning on my legs, stood meekly while Kalyani put it round his neck. Then Tod, Kalyani and I turned back the way we had come, and with Woolly walking between us we set off back along the path.

Lohrimani village school is a small building on the outskirts of the village. It is actually the first, or the last building you pass. Only a few years ago the school was the home of a popular Buddhist priest who had established a small tTemple in a building across the road. He was murdered late one night by a group of men who came to his house.

As we reached the school that day Kalyani had a brainwave.

"We'll put Woolly in the school," she said, "and when school's finished the children can walk him back to the village."

Great idea. It was still early, and the children hadn't arrived yet, so we went in and found a classroom. Woolly didn't seem at all bothered, so we tied his rope to a desk, gave him a hug, and left him there. He settled down.

We waited around outside for a teacher, so that the unexpected presence of a large dog sitting amongst the children in class wouldn't come as too much of a shock.

We didn't have long to wait. We'd met the young teacher before, and when we explained about Woolly he barely raised an eyebrow.

"No problem," he said.

How cool is that? Wonder what a teacher in England would have said?

Relieved, we set off again towards the mountain path, giggling at the thought of Woolly spending the day in a classroom.

Our last climb up the mountain was the easiest for me, and I hardly had to pause for breath at all. We reached the Village of the Damned in record time.

By chance we saw Woolly's new 'mum' there, she was in the village on an errand. Kalyani went over and spoke to her, and we saw her begin to laugh. She turned and said something to her friends and they all roared with laughter.

"I told her she could pick Woolly dog up from the school on her way home," Kalyani said. "She thought it was really funny that you'd taken the dog to school! And when I told her 'Tod says you'll have to carry Woolly's school books for him', she couldn't stop laughing! They want to know if you do things like this in England!"

The next day we travelled back to Kathmandu, and after a couple of days there we flew back to the UK.

We were so sad to leave Nepal, and the villagers who had made us so welcome during our stay. We have wonderful memories of our time there, and intend to return in the not-too-distant future.

Should you be walking through the remote Everest region of Nepal one day, and you happen upon a small village, you will know you've found Salle if the villagers run to greet you waving their arms, laughing and shouting 'Bye bye, bye bye'.

If any doubts remain in your mind, and you manage to find your way through the forest to the Junior school, stand at the edge of the trees above the school, and listen. Should you be lucky enough to hear, in the distance, the sound of children's laughter, and their voices singing the 'Hokey Cokey', then you will know for certain that you're in the right place.

'A BEARD IN NEPAL 2.
RETURN TO THE VILLAGE'

is now available.

"….a real page turner that brings joy to all its readers…."
"….sequels are a tricky thing to pull off but Fiona does so with brio…."
"….highly recommended read…."
"….the real essence of life in Nepal today has been captured by this wonderful author…."
"….can't wait for the next instalment…."

Keep up to date with Fiona Roberts' books @
www.spanglefish.com/fionaroberts

BOOKS

O is a symbol of the world, of oneness and unity. In different cultures it also means the "eye," symbolizing knowledge and insight. We aim to publish books that are accessible, constructive and that challenge accepted opinion, both that of academia and the "moral majority."

Our books are available in all good English language bookstores worldwide. If you don't see the book on the shelves ask the bookstore to order it for you, quoting the ISBN number and title. Alternatively you can order online (all major online retail sites carry our titles) or contact the distributor in the relevant country, listed on the copyright page.

See our website **www.o-books.net** for a full list of over 500 titles, growing by 100 a year.

And tune in to myspiritradio.com for our book review radio show, hosted by June-Elleni Laine, where you can listen to the authors discussing their books.